Praise for *The Productivity Epiphany*

"*The Productivity Epiphany* provides a steady stream of thought-provoking insights you can use to ramp up your productivity in all areas of life. It's full of unusual and unpredictable insights and tools, yet written in a way that will comfortably jar your mind into new ways of perceiving and understanding. This is one book you can't afford to be without."

—Mollie Marti, Ph.D.
CEO, Best Life Design, and Author of
The 12 Factors of Business Success

"*The Productivity Epiphany* is bursting with insights that will allow you to be more productive and get more enjoyment out of life. Vince Harris shares the wisdom that is the result of hundreds of coaching sessions with his clients over the last decade—and much, much more. This book belongs in your personal development library!"

—Dr. Joe Vitale
Author of *The Attractor Factor*, www.mrfire.com

"Many specific ways to influence others, yourself, and your life! Vince has put together a life manual that cuts through the useless items that a lot of books are filled with. What you get here is a quick idea, why it works, and how to use it! Many of these ideas you can apply in the next few minutes and get a measurable result for yourself. I really like the way Vince talks in plain language that anyone can understand and therefore apply! If you are looking for that 'Life Manual' you can take with you as well as to the bank, this is it! It's a home run, Vince. Great job!"

—Harlan Goerger
President H. Goerger & Associates, Author of
The Selling Gap

"Our happiness, productivity, fulfillment, self-esteem level, charisma quotient, and ability to manifest the things most important to us are all dependent upon how we picture ourselves, others, and the world in general. If we can alter how we perceive things, we can shift our reality and experience new insights and breakthroughs in every aspect of our lives. *The Productivity Epiphany* is loaded with wisdom, new ways to see ourselves and others, and entertaining stories that allow us to see things in an entirely new and supportive light. If you are ready to experience a bunch of epiphanies of your own, this is the book for you."

—Dr. Joe Rubino
Founder, CenterForPersonalReinvention.com;
Creator, SelfEsteemSystem.com

"My humble library is simply awash with books on sales and self-improvement. I bought some of them, but most were sent by friends and acquaintances wanting an endorsement. I haven't read most of them, but I'm reading this one and I'll tell you why. It's eminently readable.

"The first thing I noticed is that there are 52 chapters populating a few more than 140 pages. My rudimentary math tells me the average chapter is about two pages long, and I can handle that. It's ideal for those few moments I can scrape out of my day, like in the bathroom, for example.

"The next thing I noticed is that it largely comprises stories, and they are *good* stories. Stories are the best way to learn.

Here's the bottom line. Books you don't read can't possibly do you any good. *The Productivity Epiphany* will help you improve your life because you will read it and enjoy it in the process."

—Hank Trisler
Author of *No Bull Selling* and *No Bull Sales Management*, both published by Bantam Books

"*The Productivity Epiphany* shows us that becoming more effective in life doesn't always come down to a single formula; huge leaps forward often result from those aha moments that seem to come from nowhere. When you read Vince's book, you'll know where your epiphanies came from!"

—Tom Antion
Past president, National Capital Speakers Association, and Author of *The Ultimate Guide to Electronic Marketing for Small Business*

"This book is jam-packed with useful tools! Vince Harris provides dozens and dozens of fascinating and practical techniques to increase our influence and effectiveness. Harris finds these tools in scientific research literature, his personal experience, or the proven experience of others, and presents them in an engaging, informative, and easy style. I was absorbed and expanded by this book. You will profit from owning, reading, and rereading this book."

—Eric S. Knowles
Emeritus Professor of Psychology, University of Arkansas; Chief Scientist, Omega Change Consulting Group; Author, *Resistance and Persuasion*

"Insightful, engaging, and informative! Vince Harris's new book *The Productivity Epiphany* is truly a blueprint on how to master your time, your relationships, and your life. The wisdom you will gain from reading this book will give you the courage to change your life and the strategies to take your life to the next level of understanding and success."

—Johnny Campbell, The Transition Man
Author of *Selling to Brand X & Y: How to Sell to Generation X & Y*, www.transitionman.com

"If you are truly ready to transcend your past limitations and create extraordinary success for your life, *The Productivity Epiphany* is the resource you need. Providing you with life-transforming information, new levels of self-awareness, and actionable strategies, it will empower you to start becoming the productive person you deserve to be!"

—"Yo Pal" Hal Elrod
Author of *Taking Life Head On!* and Cofounder of Your Best Life Coaching,
www.YourBestLifeEveryday.com

"Vince Harris has brought together a collection of advice and ideas which if applied can have a positive impact on its reader. The ideas included are presented in a way that is unique and easy to digest."

—Josh Hinds
Speaker, Author, and Entrepreneur,
www.GetMotivation.com

The productivity Epiphany

**Become more productive
in any area of life!**

The productivity Epiphany

Become more productive in any area of life!

Vincent Harris

TREMENDOUS
LIFE BOOKS.com

The Productivity Epiphany

Published by
Tremendous Life Books
206 West Allen Street
Mechanicsburg, PA 17055

ISBN: 978-1-933715-97-1

Library of Congress Cataloging-in-Publication Data
Harris, Vincent
The Productivity Epiphany: Leading Edge Ideas: Time Management, Self Management, Communication. Become More Productive in Any Area of Life! / by Vincent Harris
Library of Congress Control Number: 2008910283

Printed in the United States of America

To my daughter, Chloe,
a beautiful little girl with a brilliant mind.
There's nothing you could do to make me love you any
more, and nothing you could do to
make you love you any less.
To my wife, Valerie, I love you.

Contents

Foreword

It's the greatest challenge we all face: getting ourselves to do things we want to do, but we can't get past the inertia to build momentum . . . to actually do those things.

The second problem we face? The one that happens when we actually *do* get up the initiative, we do build momentum to face overwhelming moments . . . and weeks that tax us. What do we typically do? We tend to give up doing that which we want and revert to that which we have done.

That could be our old job, old career, old business, old anything . . . and we let go of that which is unfamiliar. Why?

We have evolved consistently over millennia to do that which keeps us alive . . . that which causes us to survive. And that is a very good thing. But there is no gene that allows for initiative. Safety, security, love, acquisition, eating, physical activity . . . yes. Initiative and stick-to-itiveness are very different. We aren't wired for it.

Instead, we are wired to be comfortable. We are wired to have enough. So we face ourselves and only ourselves. We face our most complex desires and emotions, and they don't want to move; they don't want to manage time effectively. And it is the "thinking you" who can win over your basest drives and desires.

Don't get me wrong—your drives and desires are good things. But they've been running the brain for so long that the brain forgot it could take control.

The brain can consciously help you lose weight, get things done, and—in general—change. Consciousness is strong, but nonconsciousness usually wins out because conscious strength needs to be trained to win the "friendly bat-tle" with the no-conscious.

Vince Harris, in this brilliant new book, is going to show you how to do just that.

I'm delighted that you have taken the initiative today.

My hat is off to you, and I am excited for you as you begin this wonderful journey.

Kevin Hogan, Psy.D.
Author of *The Psychology of Persuasion*

Acknowledgments

My parents, Jerry Harris and Cheryl Mclain, first and foremost, got me here. They successfully did the toughest job around; they made sure I made it from infancy to adulthood in one piece, and believe me, I didn't make that an easy task. To my parents, I love you.

In the summer of 1976, a neighbor and family friend, Wayne Brassfield, gave me a tattered copy of the classic self-help book *Think and Grow Rich*. To say that this single decision by Wayne changed my life would be an understatement. But then again, that's just Wayne. He's made a habit of positively impacting the lives of young people. Thank you, Wayne.

In 1980 Bob Timmons, the track coach for the Kansas Jayhawks and mentor to Jim Ryun, took the time to write and send me two inspirational letters. They came at a time when I really needed them. Somehow, I think he knew that. One evening, some twenty-six years after I had received the last of those two letters, I called him to say, "Thank you!" It was an emotional evening for both of us.

Introduction

"An artist's duty is rather to stay open-minded and in a state where he can receive information and inspiration. You always have to be ready for that little artistic Epiphany."
—Nick Cave

"Epiphany: (1): a usually sudden manifestation or perception of the essential nature or meaning of something; (2): an intuitive grasp of reality through something (as an event) usually simple and striking; (3): an illuminating discovery, realization, or disclosure b: a revealing scene or moment."

Can you recall the last time you experienced an epiphany? In that moment, the physical boundaries that usually define where your sense of self begins and ends vanish into thin air. You feel connected to some vast storehouse of wisdom that has suddenly allowed you to understand the solution to some issue that seemed insurmountable.

What is most surprising, perhaps, is the fact that the trigger for our epiphanies often has no apparent logical connection to what we've been seeking to resolve. Here lies the secret. Because we are thinking about something that has no correlation to our problem, the filters that keep us fixated on the problem have temporarily ceased to exist. Our open-mindedness lets the information slip past the gatekeeper of our mind, sliding like some ethereal skeleton key into our mental deadbolt. Then, with one easy turn—*click*—the door swings wide open.

The Productivity Epiphany was written to provide you

with stories, insights, and strategies that give you the opportunity to experience your own epiphanies. Unlike most books that move cleanly from one section to the next, I have gone to great lengths *not* to arrange this book that way. Predictability allows us to prejudge; we anticipate the content of the next chapter or section of a book, and this all but guarantees that only a limited amount of the information will get through.

During the last decade I have consulted for men and women who were looking for some kind of breakthrough in their life. The time I spent with my clients has taught me far more than I ever imagined. All of my clients have taught me something of value. Much of what they have taught me is presented here.

How many epiphanies will you experience as you read *The Productivity Epiphany?* That's the best part. I can't know, and neither can you. You may have many, or you may only have one . . . initially. As the circumstances of your life change, new epiphanies await where none had existed before.

You may see the same concept presented more than once, in a similar, but clearly different format. When you do, it is not a mistake. We learn more when we encounter the same idea from slightly different perspectives.

Reading *The Productivity Epiphany* is like an archaeological dig. You'll find some real treasures just beneath the surface; you may not immediately know just what to do with some of those treasures, or until later that you've even discovered a treasure. When the excavation is complete, you will realize that you have uncovered far more than you could have ever hoped for. Those treasures won't come *from* this book; they'll come from within *you.*

I wish you many epiphanies, and I know you'll use your new awareness to take your life to a whole new level.

Chapter 1

Effortlessly Bypassing Resistance

"One man's ways may be as good as another's, but we all like our own best."
—Jane Austen

"Look, what you need to do is just quit eating so much and start exercising!" Have you ever had someone say something like this to you? Did it motivate you? Probably not. In fact, you probably did the exact opposite. Research shows that many of us do things that are counterproductive to get back at those who have hurt us emotionally.

What's the solution when we want someone to follow our advice? If presented in a way that does not trigger a defensive response in our listener, the information is more easily, and willingly, processed.

I invite you to consider something that happened to me several years ago. One morning I went to put on a pair of pants that I had not worn for a few months. I noticed that the pants were now a little too tight around my waist. I said to myself, *You have to start exercising more and eating healthier!*

Now, if you look back at this last paragraph, you will see that I began by *inviting* you to *consider* something. I did not tell *you* to exercise more and eat healthier; I just told *you* what I said to *myself.* Packaged like this, you get to hear the same message, but it does not make your authority-figure alarm go off. It does not make you dismiss a message that may be beneficial to you.

21

This is delivering a message under the analytical radar. Why would you resist listening to something I said to myself? You wouldn't. But by listening to me talk about what I said to myself, you get to decide whether or not it is something that would also benefit you. It's a sneaky way of planting a suggestion as a seed that, given the proper environment, can sprout into a productive behavior.

I have assisted countless business leaders and professionals in speaking more precisely. Initially, they are skeptical; they always wonder how just a few simple changes in how they word things can bring about such a dramatic change. But after they have experienced the results firsthand they never again talk as they once did.

Formula for Delivering Suggestions under the Radar
1. Think about the thought, idea, or suggestion on which you would like the listener to take action.
2. Place the suggestion in the form of something you said to yourself or something that was said to you.

Example
I want someone to start getting their reports completed and turned in a little faster. The suggestion might be, *"Get your reports done faster or things could get ugly."*

I might tell a story like this: "John, I'll never forget some of the lessons I learned the hard way when I first started with this company twenty years ago. There were so many little things I was doing wrong that eventually were going to put my job in jeopardy. We had this crotchety old manager named Bill Smith, and I'll never forget the day he walked up to me, got right up in my face, pointed his finger at me and said, *'Young man, I suggest you get your reports done faster or things could get ugly!'* What do you think I did? That's right, I took his advice, and things at work started getting better immediately." By hiding the suggestion in what someone else told you, you dramatically reduce the likelihood of John getting defensive. Because he feels like it was his idea, he actually feels good about himself when he gets his reports completed in a timelier manner; it creates a self-reinforcing loop of success.

You'll be surprised at what you can say to other people without causing their alarms to go off. In fact, I often say to myself, *You're off your rocker if you don't use the power of placing suggestions inside of quotes when talking to other people!*

As you are delivering the quote, adopt the body language and tone of voice of the person whom you are describing. In the example I used, you would actually get closer to the person you are telling the story to, point your finger at the person, and deliver the message using a crotchety-old-man voice. This action will feel strange the first few times you try it. But remember, people won't be mad at you. You're just telling them what someone else said and did, and that's exactly how they'll process it consciously.

A mentor of mine perhaps said it best: "Use this at least five times a day for the next two weeks, and you'll find that people respond to you in an entirely different way."

Chapter 2

You Better Get That Chip *on* Your Shoulder

*"The authentic self is the best part of a human being.
It's the part of you that already cares, that is already
passionate about evolution. When your authentic self
miraculously awakens and becomes stronger than
your ego, then you will truly begin to make a difference in this world. You will literally enter into a part-
nership with the creative principle."*
—Andrew Cohen

When you were a child, you no doubt heard the phrase,
"He's got a chip on his shoulder!" This usually had a negative connotation, referencing an arrogant and combative
attitude. I'm going to suggest that having a chip on your
shoulder can be a reason to celebrate.

Some years ago I read a fantastic little eBook titled *The
Self-Esteem Book,* by Dr. Joe Rubino. I can't recommend
this book enough. Dr. Rubino introduces a funny-looking
little character named Chip. This imaginary creature is the
representative of our negative inner dialogue. We are told
that he spends his time riding on our shoulder, spewing nonsense and negativity in our ear. Until we understand that
Chip is not the real us, we mistake his non-sense as insight
from the wise part of ourselves. The concept of Chip has the
ability to change your life. When you begin to perceive the
negative chatter as something that comes from outside of
you, from a freaky-looking entity that wants to make you

feel terrible, you will make massive, immediate shifts in your positive self-awareness.

Realizing how brilliant Dr. Rubino's concept was, I asked myself, *How could I use this with my clients?* If you take a moment to think about it, when we are connected to what I call our true essence, we often feel warmth, or certain pleasurable sensations in our chest or abdomen. In fact, if you just move your awareness to the area around your heart for a moment, you'll notice a shift in your breathing and a feeling of tranquility following right behind. Did you feel it? Why is this important?

Noticing that the internal garbage is not really you makes a huge difference, just by itself. However, if you immediately shift your awareness to the location of your true essence, the effect is amplified to immeasurable degrees. After guiding clients into a deeply relaxed state, I assist them in the process of making these shifts of awareness—and thus a shift in states of mind and body—by strategically using Chip and the true essence zone.

The moment you decide to start picturing negative internal chatter as coming from a funny-looking little creature that rides on your shoulder, you'll start to grant those comments the power they deserve: *none.* When you want to connect with the part of you that truly does have your best interest in mind, take your awareness to the area surrounding your heart, and listen to what you hear. You'll find great wisdom in the information you receive.

Get Dr. Joe Rubino's free audio,
"7 Steps to Soaring Self Esteem," at
www.selfesteemsystem.com

Chapter 3

Stop! There Was Not a Gorilla on the Court

"Focus on your potential instead of your limitations."
—Alan Loy McGinnis

Let me ask you a question. Do you think you would notice a gorilla on the court during a basketball game? Not if you were doing the task that subjects at the University of Illinois were asked to do.

When I'm assisting someone suffering from chronic pain, I'm often asked, "How is learning to think in a different way going to help my pain? My pain is real; it's not just in my mind!" To answer this, let's focus on the power of our attention and what role this can play in our experience of pain.

Our attention acts as a filter, a very powerful filter! Daniel Simons and Christopher Chabris conducted a study on this subject at the University of Illinois that had shocking results. The subjects were asked to watch a video of a basketball game and were tasked with just one thing: they were asked to count the number of passes made by the players wearing the white shirts.

At one point during the video, someone in a gorilla suit walked through the game and stood in the middle of the screen before walking slowly off the court. Over half of the subjects did not see the gorilla, a gorilla that was obviously not a normal part of the context.

When the subjects had their attention riveted on the players, their brain deleted the things that didn't match what they had been asked to observe, even when those things were right in front of their face. Whenever I have a client who has an overactive conscious mind, I utilize this principle and overload their conscious mind with other tasks.

A statement I make in the initial session is, "Let's get this out of the way now; I can't make you *do* anything!" Many times people ask, "Can you make me stop smoking?" I respond with, "Oh, believe me, I could. Let me put a gun to your head, and I guarantee you will stop smoking. But that's not my line of work."

I remind them that I am a coach with tools and skills, but I am only able to unleash the resources they already have. I am an active participant in a teaching process—the process of learning to use your brain to do phenomenal things.

Our attention is always on something! Where we choose to place our attention creates the largest part of our reality. We tend to see and experience more of what we are focused on, good or bad. Isn't it true that the last time you bought a new car, dress, or suit, you started seeing similar items everywhere? They were there before you bought them, but the new relevancy in your life shifted your attention, bringing what had always been there into your current awareness.

Mastering the skill of shifting your attention can be one of the most empowering tools you will ever use. A big part of what I do involves teaching people how to begin mastering this skill. I can assist people in not seeing, hearing, or feeling certain things, so they can focus on seeing, hearing, and feeling other things. Everyone can learn this. In fact, everyone is already doing it daily, just not in a way that serves them well.

So don't be so sure that you could never miss a gorilla on the basketball court. More important, how many gorillas are you missing because of your habitual focus of attention?

Chapter 4

You Could Live Like a King, But Why Stoop to That Level?

"The manager has a short-range view; the leader has a long-range perspective."
—Warren Bennis

Were you aware that you have been living better than a king? I didn't know that for a long time, but after I realized it, every aspect of my life blossomed with new meaning.

We make comparisons all day long. Some are made consciously, but most are made outside of our conscious awareness. The question is (and, oh, what a big question it is), what are we making our comparisons to?

Recently, I had a conversation with my eighty-year-old great-aunt about a power outage she had experienced for four hours earlier that day. Our conversation eventually led to discussing what life had been like during her youth.

Until she married, she didn't have electricity in her home. Fires were started three times each day to cook, even when the August heat was already pushing the inside temperature to 100 degrees Fahrenheit. Butter and milk were kept cool by placing them in a bucket and lowering them down into the well.

Now, go back in time a few hundred years and pick any king from that period. Wouldn't you agree that even my great-aunt had more luxuries than the most powerful man in the land a few hundred years before? When we learn to ask ourselves what we are comparing something to, our attitude begins to shift.

A study was once conducted to determine why some injured athletes can return to their career while others seem to crumble. Those who had a successful recovery were found to have made self-to-self comparisons. In other words, they compared where they are today with where they were last week. Conversely, those who never really recovered were caught up in making self-to-*other* comparisons. They looked at where they were compared to where someone else was in their recovery.

You may be wondering if self-to-other comparisons are always a poor choice. The achievements of others serve as wonderful examples of what has been possible for people to accomplish. The danger with these examples can be found when we perceive a wide gap between what we believe this other person can do, and what we believe *we* can do.

Below is a list of the six keys to successful athletic rehabilitation and a positive mental attitude. Please notice that these same keys can be used with great success in most any other area of life.

- Inner motivation
- The value of high standards
- Breaking goals into smaller chunks
- A flexible time frame
- Personal involvement/taking responsibility
- Self-to-self comparisons

You may find that reflecting from time to time on these six key areas allows you to mentally review your life and determine where you may be off track. This review allows you to take action and get your train rolling once again.

Chapter 5

Radio Station K-BAD MOOD

"Our appearance is a powerful communication tool, sending messages to every sighted person. Everyone is highly influenced by the visual impression of a person they are meeting for the first time."
—Catherine Bell

Have you ever been in a bad mood for no apparent reason? There is a very strong possibility that it could be related to what you have been reading or what radio station you have been listening to.

In a recent study involving our moods, John Bargh, Mark Chen, and Lara Burrows made a game that involved a scrambled sentence test. Subjects were given a scrambled sentence of fifteen words, and then had to make as many fifteen-word sentences with those words as they could. One group was given words that had to do with poor behavior: words like "intrude," "aggressively," and "sarcastic." The neutral group was given very neutral words. The polite group had words such as "kind," "joyful," and "cooperative."

The subjects didn't know there were different versions of the test and had no idea what the real purpose of the study was. Each subject had about five minutes to do the puzzle. The crucial point came when subjects walked out of the room to inform the proctor that they had finished the test. By design, the proctor would always be talking to someone else as each person finished the test. What happened next was what really interested the researchers. They wanted to know one thing: would the subject interrupt? The results are very revealing.

Only 15 percent of those who had been doing the puzzles with polite words interrupted within ten minutes. Those who had been using poor-behavior word puzzles had a 60 percent interrupt ratio in the same ten-minute period.

This technique is called the Velten Procedure. This method was developed in the 1960s and has unlimited possibilities for personal development. This experiment shows that by simply having someone work with certain words for a few minutes, behavior can be predictably influenced.

Our moods are heavily influenced by what we read, who we hang out with, the music we listen to, and countless other things in our daily surroundings. Unless we increase our awareness, we don't even have a say in whether or not to accept the influence. Once we are in a foul mood, our mood taints everything else we encounter. If you think someone is going to be rude to you, you become rude first, and then infect the other person with your mood. It's really scary how easily we push other people into roles without realizing it, and thus our own predictions are confirmed.

During this week, pay attention to the music you play. Do you listen to songs about divorce, sadness, hangovers, and hard times? Is it possible that you could be setting your thoughts in the wrong direction each morning?

Have you ever been told, "You should never judge a book by its cover"? Here is something you may want to consider; people *do* judge a book by its cover, and more important, they judge you by yours.

How many political figures do you see with facial hair? Almost none. There is a reason: people tend to distrust those with facial hair. I have found that people treat me more favorably when my face is clean-shaven than when I have a goatee. However, I want to show you something far more compelling.

Dr. Andrew Harrell from the University of Alberta has shown that attractive kids are physically abused and murdered less often by their mothers than unattractive kids. Just as shocking, only 1.2 percent of the least attractive children were buckled in their car seats, while 13.3 percent of the attractive children were strapped in for safety. The point is clear; if physical attractiveness influences parents to treat *their own children* differently, then we cannot pretend that its power is anything less than astonishing.

The clothes we wear, the style of our hair, our posture, our voice, and our gestures all help to create the image that shows others who we are. So forget about debating whether it's fair or not. That is not relevant. The fact is, people *do* judge us by our appearance, and we all have a say in how others perceive us, by the decisions we make about how to present ourselves.

Take some time this week and watch how often what people wear influences the way you respond to them. You will be amazed! If you really want to have fun, go into a jewelry store in your best outfit. Just walk in, and take note of how you are treated. Go back at some later date wearing old jeans and a ratty T-shirt, and notice how you are treated then. If it is anything like the experiments I have conducted, you will never again doubt the power of your appearance.

Chapter 6

The Most Important Third of Your Life

"Crude classifications and false generalizations are the curse of organized life."
—George Bernard Shaw

I was diagnosed with fibromyalgia in 1997. I can still vividly remember my constant search for the latest, greatest, miracle pain-relieving product, the one that would eliminate the need for any effort on my part. I probably purchased every product on the market between 1996 and 1998 that promised to banish the pain. But something happened in 1998 that would forever change my life.

In December 1998 I completed a course that helped me to learn about unlocking the part of my mind that would allow me to eliminate, regulate, or modify my pain and discomfort.

One concept I learned is the idea that chronic pain consists of one-third remembered pain, one-third actual pain, and one-third anticipated pain. Each third contributes to the overall gestalt we erroneously refer to as constant pain. Understandably, this model is particularly useful, as two-thirds of this gestalt does not exist outside of the life that we give it.

When one is able to stop the frequent replays of past moments of pain, that person eliminates one-third of the experience of discomfort. Likewise, when a person learns how to derail the worry about how much hurt will be expe-

33

rienced in the future, another third of the pain is eradicated.
Before you dismiss this concept as nonsense, let's take a
look at it from a neurological perspective that nearly everyone has experienced countless times already. Since most of
us don't have a life history void of pain or injury, we can
identify with much of what we see others endure.

The directors of horror movies rely on this mechanism to
make us scream when we watch the poor victim on screen
get stabbed in the eye with a screwdriver. While you've
probably been fortunate enough to escape the screwdriver-
in-the-eye dilemma, you have most likely inadvertently
poked yourself in the eye; you have a memory of discom-
forting experiences with your eye, and that's enough to
cause you to squirm just by watching alternative uses for
screwdrivers.

When I was in the throes of my fibromyalgia, I would
wake up each day knowing how bad I would feel after I got
out of bed (anticipating future pain). I knew this because
that's how I had felt yesterday and countless days prior
(remembering past pain). Interestingly enough, anticipating
pain and remembering pain both contribute to the present
moment. When we learn to experience only what is present,
we find that we have significantly transformed our reality.

If you are willing to take this concept and apply it to your
own experience of pain (physical, mental, emotional, or otherwise), you will no doubt discover applications that reach
far beyond the examples I've given here.

Chapter 7

Saying Hello without Saying a Word

"If you wish your merit to be known, acknowledge that of other people."
—Unknown

When we hear someone say, "He is an excellent communicator," we usually think of someone with strong verbal skills. While linguistic skills serve a vital role in effective communication, we can increase our communication and persuasion skills by learning how to consciously use communication tools that, for the most part, are unconscious behaviors.

When meeting someone for the first time, long before we are close enough to shake hands, we have the opportunity to trigger something deep inside their mind; we can trigger the part of their brain that says, "I feel good about you!"

Scientists have long known about a powerful nonverbal expression that acts as an invitation for interaction, and that subtly but powerfully lets the other person know that you recognize them. The eyebrow flash is a behavior that is seen in every culture; whether it's tribesmen from the Amazon or someone from any other culture on our planet, men, women, and children have been observed quickly raising and lowering their eyebrows when recognizing someone with whom they're acquainted.

A good way to bring this more fully into your conscious awareness is to simply watch other people. More specifically, watch how people react to seeing someone they recognize. Realize that the people you are watching usually have no conscious awareness of sending or receiving the eyebrow flash; they are simply responding to this signal unconsciously.

Knowing that we automatically deliver the eyebrow flash when we see someone we know and how powerfully this signal impacts those we deliver it to, we can choose to use it for a different purpose.

Let me suggest that you begin using the eyebrow flash with people you don't yet know, but would like to. Use it from a distance of at least six feet, and up to as far away as someone can visually register the signal—say across a room, or from the other end of an aisle in a grocery store.

I often walk through the grocery store eyebrow flashing anyone who happens to make eye contact with me. The result is nothing short of amazing; people smile, and I can observe them physically relaxing their posture, often initiating a conversation with me.

The eyebrow flash is very fast, consisting of a rapid rise and fall of the eyebrows, followed by a smile.

A word of warning: The eyebrow flash is such a powerful unconscious signal that unless you want to send a message of a potentially hostile interaction, you should always respond to the eyebrow flash initiated by others by acknowledging them, too.

Chapter 8

Forget about Becoming Bilingual; You Better Become Trilingual

"Good communication is as stimulating as black coffee, and just as hard to sleep after."
—Anne Morrow Lindbergh

Can you imagine showing up at a seminar, only to discover that the presenter is using a language that you don't understand? Unless you speak Mandarin Chinese, listening to a speaker using this language will be of little use in terms of learning something new.

I'd like to talk a bit about something that's generally not thought of as a language per se, but has the power to captivate effortlessly. Each person has a preferred way of listening to the verbal world around them. Imagine for a moment that you have been given three different screens, each about the size of a house window screen, with a wooden handle attached.

Now, pretend that a new law requires that when someone is talking, you must choose one of the screens and hold it up in front of your face. The purpose of the screen is to filter the words being spoken to you. Each screen has a different filtering function.

The first one allows only visual-related words to come through—words and phrases like "I *see* what you mean," "It was so *bright*," and "the deepest *red* I had ever *seen*."

The second one allows only words associated with

sounds—auditory words like "I *hear* what you're *saying*," "*Sounds* good to me," and "That *rings* a *bell*"—to come through.

The third screen only allows words and phrases to come through that are associated with feelings, such as, "I just need to get a *grip* on things," "It *felt* as though the sun was *warming* me right *down* to my *bones*," and "There was a *heavy feeling* in the room."

Each person's brain has developed the cognitive equivalent of just such a screen. Rather than noticing that other screens are available, we tend to rely on just one. Thus, our experience of the world is then filtered through that one conceptual screen.

When I am in a room that has a television on, I immediately stop what I'm doing and direct my attention to the television if someone pauses on the Discovery Channel; the Discovery Channel is full of things I'm interested in, and noticing the Discovery Channel logo on the bottom of the screen says to my brain, "Hey, this is stuff you like!" Let the person with the remote flip to a cooking channel, and I'm right back to my previous project; a cooking channel is the wrong channel for capturing my attention.

When speaking to just one person, the strategy is simple; we listen for the preferred channel that person uses and then construct our message to that person, using that chosen channel. If, for example, someone said to me, "Jim called the other night and he was really *down*. I just *felt* like he needed a *lift* or something. You know, we just never know the *burden* that others are *carrying* on their *shoulders*," I would reply in their obvious channel preference of feelings, or the kinesthetic mode: "Oh, yes, that's *heavy* stuff. I mean, sometimes we just can't seem to *grasp* that we always have others who would *lend* a helping *hand*, and who would be glad to make our life a little *lighter*."

In the above example, the other person would feel very

connected to me and the message I deliver. If, instead, I would have said, "I *see* what you mean. *Look*, sometimes we just don't have a *vision* that keeps us *looking* forward, when all we really need is to understand that there's someone out there who can *brighten* our day," we might as well be from another galaxy. Neurologically speaking, it's like a foreign language.

Right now you might be thinking, *But not everyone has the same channel, so what good is this when I'm speaking to a group of people?* You are exactly right. You typically have people with all of the channel preferences, so you have to become trilingual.

As you learn to weave the words and phrases of the three major preferences into your presentations, you'll find that people are leaning forward on the edge of their seats when you speak. An example of this trilingual approach of presenting would be, "So ladies and gentlemen, as you *envision* a future with the people around you who *support* your mission, *saying* things to yourself like, 'It *feels* so good to have so many people *behind* me,' you'll *see* just how good it can *feel* to have people *telling* you that you *will* make it."

To become masterfully proficient with this skill, think of a message you would like to deliver, and then construct it for each of the different channels. After you have written the three separate messages, blend them all into one. While you won't master this skill overnight, you will be amazed at how quickly you begin to notice how others use the preferred channel words and phrases. Allow this awareness to expand each day, continually incorporating more of the preferred words of others into your own communication. Don't be surprised if the knowledge of channel preferences finds its way into your relationships at home, too. What language does your significant other speak, or your children? Once you know, you'll be able to deepen those relationships. Have fun.

Chapter 9

They Lied about Pride

"Besides pride, loyalty, discipline, heart, and mind, confidence is the key to all the locks."
—Joe Paterno

Many of us were raised to believe that pride was a good thing; we often heard things like, "He's a good man; the guy's got a lot of pride!" When we are seeking to build our self-esteem on a solid foundation, however, we may want to look a little closer at this "pride" creature.

Perhaps the most easily recognized sign of low self-esteem is pride. Does that shock you? Pride is a feeling that derives from things from the outside. People who constantly profess their pride in college degrees, addresses, careers, and such are always comparing themselves to others and looking at the things they have. Interestingly enough, these people usually don't think too highly of themselves.

"Is it wrong to be proud of myself?" you may ask. Of course not; listen to that question closely, though. There is a big difference in being proud for earning the degree and having pride in the degree. Simply knowing that you earned the degree and then feeling good about it are sufficient for feeling good about yourself. Pride, however, is not satisfied to remain quiet within; pride needs fuel from the attention of others to stay alive.

The glue that holds pride together is that of comparison;

you must compare yourself to someone you know does not measure up to you.

Self-esteem, on the other hand, is something that comes from within; you feel good about who you are on the inside, and you feel good about your situation at any given point on your journey of achievement. People with pride feel good about themselves when they have finally earned their Ph.D.s (they think), while people with strong self-esteem feel good about themselves every step of the way. While people may look forward to the benefits of having their Ph.D., they are as comfortable with themselves while working on their associate degree as they will be when they are finally called "doctor."

When we begin to observe the difference between pride and self-esteem in others, we'll be better equipped to see this same thing in ourselves. We will know we are operating from a healthy self-esteem level when we are thinking from a mind-set of abundance. Saying hateful things to or about others, making comparisons to other people, and looking for our security in our outer wolrd are all signs that we are functioning from the position of pride.

Awareness is the key that releases us from this mentally constructed jail cell of misery. Stay awake, stay the course, and watch your world change.

Chapter 10

Do Not Imitate Custer's Last Stand

"Let no man imagine that he has no influence.
Whoever he may be, and wherever he may be
placed, the man who thinks becomes a
light and power."
—Henry George

We all know what happened to Custer, right? It wasn't pretty. As a speaker, salesperson, manager, or parent, you never want to "die" in front of those you wish to influence, but if you take the wrong stand you may very well end up "scalped" like Custer's men.

An overwhelming body of research on covert influence shows that it really does matter where we stand when we present information to others. But if you're anything like me, research only serves as a good starting point—never a place to end.

To satisfy yourself that the position of your body in relationship to others is important, recruit several friends and ask them to help you out. Place two chairs face to face, just about three to four feet from each other. Now, assuming you are sitting in one, slide the other over about two feet to the right, so that when the other person is sitting across from you, your right eye is aligned with theirs.

Now, have each person in turn sit across from you, and have them rate, on a scale of 1 to 10, how comfortable they are with you. Next, move your chair so that they are now across from you, but to your left. Ask them to rate you again. Do this with as many people as you can find, because the results are staggering. You'll be shocked to find that almost everyone rates you higher when you are on their right side. Research also indicates that you will be seen as more attractive from this position. Can you see how this might be beneficial?

So how do you use this information in a live presentation when talking to a large group of people?

First, when you take the stage, you'll want to stand near the center, just slightly off to the right of the audience, which will be your left. As the presentation moves forward, use both sides of the stage: the side to the right of the audience for anything you want them to associate positive feelings to, and the left side for things you want them to link to negativity.

For example, if you are presenting a product or a new idea, you'll want to stand to the audience's right when you are talking about your product or idea. Then move carefully over to their left when you talk about your competitor.

Just in case you are wondering how powerful this is, when researchers placed goggles on test subjects that only allowed them to see off to their left, nearly all of them reported feelings of fear and panic. When the subjects wore goggles that only allowed them to look to their right, they felt an increased level of comfort and sense of calm.

Take a look at where you've been standing, and if you have been presenting from the audience's left, make sure your last presentation was the "last stand" in that position. If only Custer had known!

Chapter 11

Melting Resistance with Stories

"Storytellers, by the very act of telling, communicate a radical learning that changes lives and the world: telling stories is a universally accessible means through which people make meaning."
—Chris Cavanaugh

The smartest man I ever met was also the most boring. This guy had worked for NASA, and he could plow through complex computations with blinding speed. He knew a lot about everything; it didn't seem to matter what the topic of discussion happened to be; he knew something about it.

With all of this knowledge, one thing prevented him from being perceived as interesting; all he knew how to do conversationally was convey facts, and facts alone are boring. I eventually concluded that math was just one of those subjects that couldn't be fun or entertaining. Years later I met a woman who shattered the myth that math can't be fun.

Melody Shipley told stories, and these stories had embedded within them the principles a successful math student would need. I learned more after four weeks with Melody at North Central Missouri College than I had in fourteen weeks with the NASA whiz.

By capturing the attention of your audience, you can take them on a journey that travels through the various feelings and emotions that support the outcome you have decided would be beneficial for their needs. Most people tell a story with no outcome in mind. I used to be the epitome of telling irrelevant stories that left friends and family wondering what the point was. Several years ago, I was asked, "What do you want the other person to learn from this story?"

Once I finally learned to ask that question, it was like someone had greased my wheels. No longer did I feel any resistance from my listeners. I watched as people followed me from one mood shift to the next. It all started with capturing their attention.

How do you do that consistently? Talk about something controversial without taking a side. For example, "Has anyone noticed that there seems to be some conflict about why our weather is changing and if this has anything to do with global warming."

Your audience doubtlessly has strong feelings about this topic and will, therefore, be generous with its attention. Now all you have to do is keep it. How? By asking, "What could this debate have to do with why I'm here today?" You then tell them, "As I talk to you today, you'll become aware of the correlations between X and the global warming debate." As long as you provide them with something that makes a connection between the two, they'll feel the closure they need, and what you talked about will still be in their mind tomorrow.

In 1986 I received training to use what Dr. Eric Knowles refers to as Alpha Strategies. In short, Alpha Strategies are techniques designed to overcome resistance. I've also been fortunate enough to spend some time with Dr. Knowles discussing what he calls the Omega Strategies.

One technique that I absolutely love is that of simply acknowledging resistance. In one example, Dr. Knowles found that when one of his research participants asked another student, "Would you mail this letter for me?" about 70 percent of those asked said yes. However, when the assistant made the same request, but first stated, "I know you probably don't want to, but . . . ," it jumped to almost 100 percent.

If you've ever been involved in a career that requires a significant amount of persuasion, this approach will initially feel like using your nondominant hand for writing. But after you have witnessed this principle melt away resistance, you'll find yourself using it with ease.

Notice that when using this principle of acknowledging resistance, the essential message has not changed or become more attractive. You are simply letting other people know that you realize they may not want to do it, believe it, or accept it.

One caveat: Only use this tactic with something for which you are certain there will be resistance. Dr. Knowles found that when resistance was acknowledged when there was none, it could actually cause someone to doubt what you're saying.

I remember Dr. Knowles saying, "I know this seems so straightforward and simple that you may be hesitant to use it, perhaps even wanting to disregard it completely, but the science is there. . . . This stuff is powerful and will increase your persuasiveness in virtually any environment."

Chapter 12

The Power of Praise

"A desire to be observed, considered, esteemed, praised, beloved, and admired by his fellow is one of the earliest as well as the keenest dispositions discovered in the heart of man."
—John Adams

I just love it when I'm surprised by simplicity. With new discoveries being made daily, and technological advances in almost every field of study imaginable, it seems logical that if we just wait a little longer we'll have access to the be-all, end-all influence technique.

What would it be like if you discovered that you already possess the knowledge and ability to do what science has proven to be the most effective concept for influencing men? Even if you work in the female-oriented Victoria's Secret, statistics show a major percentage of sales are to men. Do you think knowing what moves them to action could be useful?

What's the last conversation you had with someone that left you feeling good about yourself? Isn't it true that when someone has praised you, complimented you, or acknowledged you in some way, it warmed you from the inside out and made you stand a little taller?

Anyone who has read Kevin Hogan's best-selling book *The Psychology of Persuasion* (a book *everyone* should own) knows that some amazingly powerful techniques for influencing and persuading others have been discovered in recent years. He told me the one thing that supersedes everything else when it comes to influencing men: praise. That's right; your chances of influencing a man go up exponentially when you sincerely deliver ample amounts of praise.

When Kevin Hogan introduced me as a speaker at his Influence Boot Camp in Las Vegas, he said, "I've coached scores of public speakers in my career. Every now and then, someone comes along who makes me stop and say, 'Wow!' I've had four or five of those people over the years. Vince Harris is one of them."

He wasn't using some intricate language pattern or complex persuasion strategy. Yet in that moment, if Kevin would have been selling cheap versions of the once-famous Pet Rock, I'd have been first in line to buy one.

None of us like to feel we are being persuaded; we do, however, like to feel good about ourselves. When the person who helps us do so also happens to have a product or service for sale, we usually repay them for their kind words, or, more precisely, *our* good feelings.

To be sure, some amazing strategies are available to move others to action. They should all be used where appropriate, but they are far more effective when used with praise. It's easy to throw a big rock through a window, but when that window has already been cracked, even the smallest of pebbles gets the job done.

Chapter 13

The Consequences of the Britney Spears Buzz Cut

"An individual's self-concept is the core of his personality. It affects every aspect of human behavior: the ability to learn, the capacity to grow and change. A strong, positive self-image is the best possible preparation for success in life."
—Dr. Joyce Brothers

Almost everyone remembers the media blitz when Britney Spears shaved her head. While I don't have any insight into Britney's reasoning, I can comment on how something as simple as shaving one's head can serve as the spark for lasting personal change.

Few things contribute to what we accomplish in life, or not, as much as our identity. Behind nearly every lasting change you'll find an identity shift that serves as the glue that holds the transformation together. Very few people have the tenacity required to maintain behavioral changes without the rock-solid foundation that a change in identity offers.

Have you ever wondered why new inductees into the armed forces have their heads shaved? It's really very simple: a person's chosen hairstyle is fused with his or her identity. For this reason, women who lose their hair while undergoing chemotherapy often describe the hair loss as the worst part of the treatment. This also explains why millions of men spend more each month on products promising to grow hair than they put into their retirement accounts.

When shearing the young recruits like so many sheep in the spring, the Army has taken a crucial step in reshaping how these young men and women perceive themselves; when there are no longer individual hairstyles and everyone looks the same, an identity vacuum results. It's much easier for the army to instill the beliefs needed to make an obedient soldier when they don't have to wrestle with an identity that may not be accepting of the principles that the military offers.

If your goal is to lose weight, rather than forcing yourself to eat less and exercise more, you first want to become the kind of person who eats only healthy foods and who can't imagine a day ending before exercising. When you begin by first adopting the identity of a person who easily and naturally eats well and exercises daily, you'll find that doing those things seem like second nature.

We can learn a great deal by looking at Hollywood. When preparing for a role in an upcoming film, actors and actresses step completely into the character they will be portraying. In fact, some of them so fully become their character that they often have difficulties breaking character. Some even require intense debriefings to get back to themselves once the film is finished. What would happen if they kept up this "pretending" indefinitely? The time would come when they would no longer identify with many of the beliefs and values that had served as their guideposts for most of their life.

With a new identity come new patterns of thinking, new patterns of behaving, and ultimately new and different results. Were the changes that resulted from Britney's shaved head in her best interest? You be the judge. One thing is certain, though. Such radical shifts in one's look often lead to new thoughts, new feelings, and in the end, new behaviors.

One final thought: If you find yourself a bit unsettled by the word "pretending" as a way of changing your identity, I invite you to consider the following.

At some point you were accepted into a certain social group. The "cool" people in those groups did and said certain things, and because you wanted to be accepted by the others, you, too, started to do those things. At first you were pretending, but eventually the behaviors became habitual unconscious behaviors.

What would happen if you pretended that you were a consistent investor? What would happen if you pretended you were a wonderful public speaker? A part of you can already sense the answer to those questions, right? Follow that inner voice, and build the identity that supports your goals.

Chapter 14

Lessons from the Hardy Women of the North

"In order to succeed, people need a sense of self-efficacy, to struggle together with resilience, to meet the inevitable obstacles and inequities of life."
—Albert Bandura

Few things affect the quality of our lives as much as our ability to bounce back after getting knocked down. One thing in life I know to be true is that if we alter our response to stressful events, we can improve our quality of life. One study by the University of Alberta shows us that we have a reason to celebrate our ability to change.

Dr. Beverly Leipert decided to study a group of women who have always had it tough. Each of the women in Dr. Leipert's study had lived much of her life in the rugged terrain of northern British Columbia.

These women lived with a rather unique set of risk factors: the bitter cold, attitudes regarding gender, threats posed by local wildlife, and very limited resources. These risks were not sporadic; they were simply a way of life.

After Dr. Leipert compiled her findings, she discovered three main strategies that were responsible for their resilience: (1) becoming what she called "hardy," (2) creating favorable meanings or "stories" about their situation in the North, and (3) supplementing what the North had to offer.

Each of these women learned to become self-reliant; had

spiritual or religious beliefs; developed a liking for outdoor activities like camping, fishing, and skiing; learned indoor activities like painting, sculpture, or quilting; and had volunteered for various community groups and activities.

Notice that each of the actions or behaviors above were *learned* or *chosen*. The resilience they developed was not some genetic gift or spontaneous phenomenon; they had taken active roles in creating the experience of the life they were living.

Think about a pinball machine. Decide today to stop being the ball, and make the decision to become the flipper. The ball is at the mercy of everything else around it. While the flipper cannot control 100 percent of what happens, it can influence the outcome to varying degrees. How do we alter these varying degrees in our favor? Let me illustrate.

When I was in high school we had a local arcade with all of the popular video games. One kid had his name ranked number one on just about every game. Did he have some special genetic code for arcade game mastery? No, he was a "master" for one very good reason; he practiced every day of his life, and therefore refined his skills.

Once you decide to become the flipper in your life, remember that you might tilt a few times at first, but like any skill in life, you'll get better the more you play.

Look back through this chapter and take some time to think about how you can apply in your own life the three main strategies that the Northern women used. Whoever said "Old dogs can't learn new tricks" was probably a poor trainer of young dogs as well.

Chapter 15

What If Everyone Were Naked?

"Leadership is an opportunity to serve. It is not a
trumpet call to self-importance."
—J. Donald Walters

Being naked is a great status equalizer. Think about the last
time you got on an elevator. Everyone was making judg-
ments about others by looking at their clothes, jewelry, and
items they were carrying.

Some might have had well-pressed and very expensive
suits; others may have been wearing diamonds or carrying
very pricey laptop computers. Perhaps someone was wearing a work shirt with his name across the pocket, with well-
worn work boots and a tool pouch hanging from his belt.

Imagine for a moment that the next time you stepped on
an elevator everyone was naked. There were no uniforms or
suits by which to classify others—no jewelry or laptops or
tool pouches. Nothing but people. Naked people.

We all have a deep and curious nature that likes to categorize others. When we have discovered who someone is,
we conveniently place our label on them and never think
about it again. While this strategy makes relating to people
easy for us (in terms of mental energy), we must realize that
others use this same strategy to categorize us.

When a company sends someone to pick me up for a
speaking engagement, this person sees me coming off the
plane looking very sharp and knows that I will be paid hand-

somely for presenting that day. They have figured me out and have decided that I'm someone important.

However, when I go into a grocery store in my hometown, the people there still see the skinny kid who was always pushing his lawnmower through town to mow yards. The skinny kid is who I am to them. The speaking and traveling are simply what I do.

But let's get beyond being naked; let's look at the fact that we are much more than our physical bodies. You have an arm, but you're not your arm. You have eyes, but you're not your eyes. You have legs, but you're not those legs.

What and who are we then? I'm comfortable telling you that I have no clue; I am even more comfortable telling you that I know we are much more than we think we are. Because we can all begin to sense this truth when we are open to it, we can also begin to make contact with, and live more fully from, this part that comes to this awareness.

Kind of confusing, isn't it? One thing I like about it, though, is that it can be as spiritual or religious as we want it to be, or it can be as scientific and tangible as we'd like. The only thing that really matters is that you acknowledge the fact that you are more than your physical body.

This concept has proven useful for people suffering from chronic pain. After teaching people how to disassociate with their physical body, they realize that although they have an arm that is experiencing pain, they are not the pain they feel in that arm. I'm confident that you can find many uses for this in your life as well.

Chapter 16

Get to Bed Early and Behave More Ethically

"In looking for people to hire, you look for three qualities: integrity, intelligence, and energy. And if they don't have the first, the other two will kill you."
—Warren Buffet
CEO, Berkshire Hathaway

Unless you've been vacationing on another planet for the last twenty years, you are aware of the importance of sleep for optimal health. Recent findings are shedding new light on this favorite nocturnal activity.

Three years ago I was out walking my dog one evening, and a friend's father spotted me as he was driving by. He pulled over to the curb to visit and explained that he had just recently had coronary bypass surgery. "The doctor told me we needed to get it done right away, and though it was up to me, he could do it that night."

Bill continued, "I looked him square in the eye, and said, "Doc, if it's all the same to you, I think I'd rather have you cuttin' on me when you're fresh. Go ahead and schedule me as the first patient on a morning after you've had a good night's sleep!" The rest of the world doesn't necessarily share Bill's commonsense approach to open heart surgery.

Living in the high-consumption society that we do, we often find ourselves dealing with people who are trying to function after getting much less sleep than their bodies need.

To be able to meet the demands of a world that says, "But

I want it *now!*" everyone from the banker to the undertaker has had to extend their hours of business. This has left only one option for anyone who wants to spend time with loved ones, pursue hobbies, or do any other activities: sleep less. This willful act of burning the candle at both ends comes with consequences, though, and it turns out that the consequences reach further than previously thought.

A study at the Walter Reed Army Institute of Research discovered that sleep deprivation leads to a rapid and significant decline in our ability to act in accordance with our moral beliefs.

William Killgore, Ph.D., revealed that the results of the study suggest sleep-deprived individuals appear to be slower in their deliberations about moral dilemmas relative to other types of dilemmas.

While experts recommend we all get seven to eight hours of sleep a night, only you know what it takes for you to operate at peak performance. For some, that means as little as four hours a night, but others may still be ragged after anything less than nine.

How much more effective would you be as a parent if you were always fully rested? As a teacher? Coach? Employee?

Like it or not, we come up against moral dilemmas almost every day. The quality of our lives ultimately boils down to the quality of our decisions, and the quality of our decisions can be traced to our mental and emotional states.

Getting the amount of sleep your body needs is perhaps the easiest way to support your mental and emotional states.

Chapter 17

You Mean Under the Right Circumstances Any of Us Could Commit Reprehensible Acts?

"Behavior is the mirror in which everyone shows their image."
—Johan Wolfgang von Goethe

I'll never forget a conversation I had about a year ago regarding the Nazi death camps of World War II. I was in a deli eating lunch, and a television played nearby. A segment on the Holocaust had just finished, and the older man next to me said, "That was some unthinkable stuff those Germans did to the Jews!" I replied, "I won't argue with that; it's hard to imagine that many people being murdered in such a short time."

The old man shot back, "It's an evil human being—no, the brother of the devil himself—that could do such a thing." No doubt expecting me to agree with him, he stiffened as he listened to my comeback.

"I'm guessing there are one hundred people shopping in this store at the moment," I said, "and I'm betting that under similar circumstances at least half of them would have followed orders and done the same reprehensible acts that the German soldiers did!"

"You must be out of your friggin' mind!" he said in a loud voice. I calmly said, "One would like to think so, wouldn't they? Unfortunately, there's a pile of research and some landmark studies that say otherwise."

Over the next thirty minutes, I carefully presented the information I had based my comments on, and he not only grew calm, but he scratched his head and said, "I'll be darned, kid."

Are you wondering what I could have possibly said to not only defuse his anger but to actually open him up?

In 1963 Stanley Milgrim knocked the field of psychology on its head. He studied the tendency of people to obey authority figures. Milgrim was troubled by how quickly the German citizens had followed the orders of Adolf Hitler and brutally slaughtered millions of people.

Milgrim's study involved telling the participants that they would be assisting him in studying the effects of punishment on learning. At the lab, participants drew slips to see who would be the teacher and who would be the learner. It was set up so that they would all be in the role of teacher.

The learner (who was secretly working with Milgrim, and posed as a student) would be strapped into a chair that could deliver shocks when the learner made a mistake on the test. They would be seated in another room, out of view from the teachers but close enough that they could be heard. The electrified chair, while looking very real, could not deliver a shock at all. It was all a setup.

Soon after the experiment had begun, the learners started making mistakes (as they had secretly been instructed). Each time a mistake was made, the researcher would instruct the teacher to administer a shock. Although the "voltage" used started out at rather harmless levels, after just a few mistakes the voltage had been dialed up to 300 volts. At this intensity, the learners were yelling in anger and pounding on the walls.

At this point the teachers would begin looking to the research person for guidance. Yet, when they did, they were simply asked to deliver yet another shock, but at a higher voltage. Each time they would seek advice or support, the researcher firmly suggested that they go ahead and give a more powerful shock to the learner.

By the time each teacher was told to stop, the voltage administered had gone all the way up to 450 volts. This is a voltage that, had it been real, clearly had the potential to kill the learners. Twenty-six of the forty teachers in the study delivered all thirty levels of shock! Many of those who delivered all thirty shocks felt a great deal of distress *about* what they were doing, but they did it anyway.

How do we explain such behavior? Milgrim concluded that when others are given instruction by a perceived authority figure, it can make very normal people do very abnormal and horrible things. Finally, Milgrim concluded that under the right circumstances any person might be capable of obeying orders to maim, injure, or even kill another human being.

The Law of Authority was alive and well in Guyana in 1978 when the nine hundred people foolishly followed the Reverend Jim Jones's orders to drink poisoned Kool-Aid.

Do you think your kids are smart enough to not take drugs when a stranger offers them? Let's hope so. However, it's not strangers we have to worry about. See, when my parents warned me about the bad things in life, I always had this image of some surly and ragged-looking bum. But that's not how it happens, is it? No, the bum often turns out to be a trusted friend or someone we have known for some time. Worse yet, it may be someone whom we see as an authority figure. For a freshman in high school, a senior on the football team may be viewed as an authority figure; it doesn't have to be a middle-aged man with a badge for the Law of Authority to prevail.

Although there are evil people in our world, sometimes decent people do evil things because they are wrongly influenced by environment and people. Teaching your children to always obey their elders may not be the best advice you can give. But the good news is that having a set of absolute values can help some people to avoid committing certain reprehensible acts.

Chapter 18

Nothing You Fear Losing Can Be the True Source of Your Happiness

"The components of anxiety, stress, fear, and anger do not exist independently of you in the world. They simply do not exist in the physical world, even though we talk about them as if they do."
—Wayne Dyer

One of the "secrets" of happiness can be found in the following question: *What would you want if you didn't have to be unhappy about not getting it?*

Let me explain a little further. Millions of people settle for far less than they are capable of, for one simple reason; they are afraid of how they would feel if they tried, but failed. Ahhh, there's that loathsome word.

We learn very little when we succeed at something, but have the potential to learn loads of valuable lessons when we fail. Please notice that I said "potential to learn." If, as was common for me in my very rebellious teens and twenties, we become angry or dejected by failure, then that potential has been wasted.

What a delightful surprise to discover that when we remain calm and collected, the pieces of the puzzle begin to fall into place, and our failure becomes the very thing we needed to be able to progress to the next step.

Here is another way of looking at this secret: *Nothing we fear losing can be the true source of our happiness.*

"But wait a minute," you may scream. "I fear losing my children, and they make me happy!" If this thought popped into your head, believe me, you're not alone. This was the very thought that had me hung up.

Have you ever heard of someone who suffered the loss of a child but went on to live a vibrant, happy life? Do you think the world is full of people like this? Just in case you don't know for sure, the answer is a resounding *yes*!

I once worked with a woman who had been experiencing a prolonged grieving period over the loss of her spouse. She was still very emotional and unable to step back into life. During our second session together, I asked her, "What would it say about you if you were no longer miserable and started enjoying life again?" She drew in a deep breath and began to cry, while breaking into a beautiful smile. "It would mean that I don't love him anymore," she said softly. That was the hard part—bringing the unconscious to the conscious. Only then could it be worked on.

If you find that you've been far too unhappy about something, or have felt a sense of continuous and ongoing unhappiness, perhaps it's time to ask yourself, *What would it mean about me if I was no longer unhappy about this?* The answer may be immediate, or it may require patience. The important thing is that after you have your answer, place it under the microscope and see if your reasons make sense.

Chapter 19

How Becoming More Productive is Like Brushing Your Teeth

"If you create an act, you create a habit. If you create a habit, you create a character. If you create a character, you create a destiny."
—Andre Maurois

About a year ago, as I was reading John Maxwell's book *Today Matters: 12 Practices to Guarantee Tomorrow's Success*, I came to a part where my mind screamed, "Go back and read that again!" What was it? *"We can't significantly change our life until we are willing to change something we do every day."*

How many times have you heard that thirty minutes of exercise three to five days a week will yield great benefits to your health? That's correct; three to five days will yield wonderful results for most people, but there's a problem built into the solution.

When we begin something that has an immediate and intense payoff, we are inclined to increase the frequency of that behavior. However, when we begin something that results in some initial discomfort, then the pendulum swings the other way for a time. The four-day-a-week early morning walk becomes three, then two, then one, and eventually you're saying, "I really need to start exercising again."

When was the last time you said, "I really need to get back into brushing my teeth"? I'm guessing you said,

"Never!" Because we were taught to brush them every day. It was neurologically wired in and became a habit that was resistant to change. It's simply inconceivable to think of *not* brushing our teeth every day.

When we do something periodically, we're sending our nervous system conflicting signals. One day we send the message of "Get used to this walk at 6:00 a.m. each day," and the next day we send the message of "Okay, nervous system, get used to sleeping in until 8:30 a.m. every morning."

So how do we do this? Do you need to start exercising? Then start walking, every single day, even if you have to start with one to three minutes a day. After only ninety days of performing a behavior, day in and day out, you have developed a habit that is as resistant to change as brushing your teeth. The more you do something, the easier it becomes, as long as no more than twenty-four hours elapses between one occurrence and the next.

Think of it: You can decide on any behavior you'd like to have as a way of life, and make it so! Forget about waiting until you feel like it; if it's not already a habit you desire, chances are you'll never feel like it. Utilize the power of acceptance to neutralize any initial resistance you might experience.

Chapter 20

You Probably Won't Believe This, But . . .

"Our age is bent on trying to make the barren tree of skepticism fruitful by tying the fruits of truth on its branches."
—Albert Schweitzer

Most of us have to communicate, on a frequent basis, with someone who refutes almost everything we say. The fact of the matter is, some people are compelled to resist. I know this because I'm a reformed resister.

Researchers are starting to ferret out important data on these knee-jerk reactions. Some of this data indicates that these reactions may have a genetic basis. My own experience has validated that my own DNA was involved in my rebellion.

I still remember coming home from school, thinking about all the things I was going to tell my parents about my day, but the moment one of them asked, "What did you do at school today?" I was compelled to clam up. It literally felt like I was being interrogated, even though they had simply asked me a question.

Recent studies have shown that some people are wired neurologically in a way that makes their sensitivity to perceived stress much higher than others. Notice, I said "perceived" stress. To the person who always resists, any information you may present is viewed as an intrusion of sorts. They experience a stress response to information that would be nonstressful to others.

The world's foremost expert on resistance reduction is University of Arkansas psychology professor Dr. Eric Knowles. He outlined several methods that have proven extremely effective for reducing resistance in others. One of them is almost embarrassingly simple.

Dr. Knowles and his colleagues discovered that by simply acknowledging the resistance, we can bring about a significant decrease in that resistance. In one study, he found that when someone was asked, "Would you mail this letter for me?" roughly 70 percent agreed. Researchers experienced an increase of 30 percent by simply inserting a short phrase just before their request. When they began by saying, "I know you might not want to, but . . . ," 100 percent of those asked said yes.

I'll share with you some ways I've incorporated this concept into my communication with clients. After I have established that the client is resisting most of what I say, I'll switch to a different mode of operation. I might say, "John, you're probably going to think what I'm going to tell you won't work, but I'm going to say it anyway, just to see what you think."

If John has previously demonstrated that his mind darts in the opposite direction, then John will be compelled to disagree with what I have just told him.

Another method I have found to be almost magical in its ability to coax others into accepting a suggestion is to extend an invitation to find the weaknesses in my ideas. "John, I know you'll most likely find this idea to be full of holes, but I'm going to ask that you analyze it carefully and note the parts that won't work." In the event that the client does resist some or all of the ideas, the version of rejection is usually much "softer." This approach helps keep the rapport between us amicable.

I'm certain that you'll find what I'm about to tell you a bit off the wall and not worthy of pursuing, but I'll tell you nonetheless; if you use this information for the next thirty days with people who have routinely resisted your ideas, you will see amazing results.

Chapter 21

We Are Equal as Far as Worth Is Concerned—And That's about It

"As we grow as unique persons, we learn to respect the uniqueness of others."
—Robert H. Schuller

We often hear parents say, "The most important thing I can give my children is my love." While this statement warms your heart initially, it may not be as reassuring as we first think. Parents do things to children every day under the guise of love—things that do little to bolster the self-esteem of these children and, in many cases, undermine the child's sense of self.

"Honey, you should be playing football, not fooling around with art. Because I love you I'm not going to let you sit in your room and work on these crazy oil paintings." A parent telling a child something like this is a clear example of how little the parent knows about human nature.

Dr. Steven Reiss, a psychology professor at Ohio State University, discovered that sixteen basic desires drive human behavior. Each of us has our own distinct profile; for each of the sixteen desires, we are driven either powerfully, moderately, or not much at all.

Dr. Reiss points out that the strength of our desires is usually formed very early in life, and while they can change as we age, our overall profile remains much the same. Why is this important? If you have a teenage boy with a low desire for physical activity and a high desire for independence, and you're trying to force him into playing football, you risk damaging your relationship and fueling the fire of resentment.

If you're wondering why parents feel compelled to push children into some things and steer them away from others, we can answer that by coming right back to the sixteen desires.

Parents with a powerful desire for status, power, and physical activity might direct their kids into activities and behaviors that match those desires. When the child in question happens to rate relatively low on those particular desires, you have a time bomb waiting to explode.

Does it seem that one of your children is your polar opposite? They may be, at least in terms of major desires. Our children will develop into strong healthy adults when we support them in activities that fulfill their sixteen desires, not ours.

Only when we understand ourselves in terms of the sixteen basic desires can we begin to more fully understand, accept, and support others. You can get a powerful overview of each of the sixteen basic desires in my audio program titled *Revealing Happiness*. For a more thorough and complete analysis I also urge you to read the book *Who Am I?* by Steven Reiss, Ph.D.

Chapter 22

What You Can Learn by Eavesdropping at McDonald's?

"We pray that the loss of life is very limited, but we fear that is not the case."
—Kathleen Blanco

A couple of weeks ago, my daughter and I were enjoying a nutrition-packed meal at McDonald's one afternoon, when I overheard one of the employees talking to someone about her recent raise. "I'm more excited about having insurance than the pay raise!" she exclaimed.

This, my friend, is at the heart of most decisions we make in life. We are motivated by both pain and pleasure, but when it comes right down to it, we'll usually do far more to avoid pain than to gain pleasure.

You probably already know that human life isn't just pain and pleasure; we are in fact motivated by at least sixteen basic desires, but for this particular section I'm just going to examine the role of pain and pleasure.

When someone needs to exercise to lose weight, but doesn't, the thought of exercising is exerting more pain than the thought of *not* exercising. The only way out of this conundrum would seem to be to eliminate the pain of not wanting to exercise, and let me tell you, I know a lot of people who fail miserably with this strategy. They convince themselves that when they get to the point that they don't wince when they think about exercise, they'll start. This is like standing on top of a big rock and trying to pick it up.

The thought of quitting smoking cold turkey when you've been a smoker for thirty years is most likely very painful, but I submit to you that no matter how much pain you're feeling, something else can always be more painful.

While working with a smoker in June 2001, I was doing my initial belief-shattering protocol with a lady who had been smoking two packs a day for nineteen years. I always start here; it's very common for someone to show up with a firm belief that they can't do it. Therefore, I always like to deal with that right off the bat. I asked her, "Will you agree to do anything I ask of you, as long as it won't cause you any harm?" She reluctantly agreed.

Even though I had no intention of having her follow through this way, I said, "I want you to quit smoking for forty-eight hours, and then we'll do your first session. It will be tough, I know, but that's the deal."

Her face revealed the obvious horror she was feeling inside. "I can't do that, Vince! There's no way; that's why I'm paying you!"

"Yes, you are paying me," I said. "Presumably because you don't know what to do anymore, isn't that right? Why don't you think you can do it?" She was digging her heels in deeper and deeper with each question I asked.

Knowing that she had a nephew who was her heart and soul, I presented her with a scenario that suddenly changed what she would be able to do. "If you walked into your house and a terrorist had Josh sitting tied up in a chair, with a gun pointed right at him, and he told you that if you smoked during the next forty-eight hours he would kill Josh, are you telling me that Josh had better be concerned?"

Tears began to stream down her face, but they were tears of realization and empowerment. She knew instantly that she did, in fact, have the ability to choose not to smoke. She knew that she'd go through hell for a few days, but to save the life of her nephew, so what? "Yes! I could go forty-eight hours!" she said in a stern voice.

I simply attached pain to something else, something much more painful. By contrast, the pain of the withdrawal became rather insignificant. After she had realized that she could gut her way through it if needed, she was ready to take a more humane approach, to work with me to eliminate the withdrawal symptoms, and to use her mind to lock the changes in place.

The pain of exercising is right now; the pain of seeing your family around your deathbed is later. Those aren't things we feel very comfortable thinking about, so we usually put them out of our mind as quickly as they come.

The McDonald's employee was more excited about having insurance—something that she'd have to get sick to use—than she was about the pay increase that she could begin using right now. Do you think pain has a significant influence in our lives? What have you been associating pain to that has been limiting you? In what way could you attach *more* pain to not doing it, which by contrast would make it seem kind of silly?

Stop trying to eliminate pain, and begin to use it with as much precision as a surgeon uses a scalpel. Make pain your friend, and many things in life suddenly become possible.

Chapter 23

Changing Beliefs with Moby Dick

"If I have the belief that I can do it, I shall surely acquire the capacity to do it even if I may not have it at the beginning."
—Mahatma Gandhi

Although complex linguistic patterns and techniques of influence work for conveying ideas to the right part of a client's brain, nothing beats letting someone physically engage in a process that ultimately allows them to discover the answer themselves.

Just around the corner from the room in which I usually see my clients is a large bookshelf that reaches from the floor to the ceiling. The only book with a red covering is *Moby Dick*, with the large black letters of the title clearly written on its spine. All of the other books are dark in color.

During a session, when the time seems right, I'll ask my client if he or she would go into the other room and get the book with the black cover, *Moby Dick*. Walking over and grabbing the book off of the shelf and returning should take less than thirty seconds, and that's being really generous.

However, at least a full minute goes by before I hear, "Are you sure it's in here?" After assuring them that it is there, I can sense their frustration building as they search in vain for the book. When I walk in the room and get the *red* book, with "Moby Dick" on the spine, the responses are all some version of "Oh my God, I saw that book. I looked right at it, but I didn't see those words on the spine!"

By telling people the cover of the book is black, I set the frame of reference for how their brain would sort as they scanned the many books this bookcase holds.

Each time their eyes would move across the red book and their brain would detect the color red, the delete function kicked in and the words "Moby Dick" did not register.

So let me ask you, what frames of reference have you instructed your brain to use for finding solutions? Have you unknowingly given your brain instructions that are the equivalent of a black-covered book?

The frame of reference we hold shapes, alters, and modifies all incoming information. The firing of Don Imus at MSNBC is a tremendous example. Soon after Imus made an unfortunate remark, a poll at MSNBC showed that almost half of the people felt that the two-week suspension was too harsh, and the other half were all but calling for him to be beheaded.

Those who felt that Imus should be fired held a frame of reference that would see or identify with only the information that matched their frame, and would delete, distort, or deny what didn't. What about those who felt he was just doing his job? Same thing: The frame these people held functioned in exactly the same way.

When you wish to persuade someone else, working (at least initially) within that person's frame of reference or metaphor produces staggering results. Trying to impose your frame upon another person's, however, only results in a war of frames.

Let's think about how we can use this knowledge to work in our own lives. What are your frames regarding marriage? Disciplining a child? Handling finances? Chances are that you know what you do regarding each of these areas, but my experience has been that very few people are aware of the frame of reference they have that drives these behaviors.

People generally reveal only half of the structure of their belief. When someone says, "Chevrolet sucks, I'd never drive one!" we really have very little to work with. When someone says something like this, just look at them and say, "Because?" You'll then get the half that they use to support their first statement. "Because I was driving back from Tulsa late one night, in a Chevy Malibu, and the thing broke down at 2:00 a.m. in the middle of nowhere!"

Knowing this, you now have countless ways to deconstruct the belief they have been using since the breakdown, and help them build another one, often in simple conversation.

One of my favorites is presenting them with a counterexample. "I'm wondering, do you think that in the history of Tulsa, there has ever been a Ford, Chrysler, Buick, or Toyota that broke down on the highway in the wee hours of the morning?"

Listing all of your first-half beliefs on one side of a piece of paper, then writing down the supporting half on the other side, could allow you to see how weak some of your supporting evidence has been.

Here's an example:

I will never be rich BECAUSE *I don't have a college degree.*

I can't lose weight BECAUSE *I don't like to exercise.*

When we allow ourselves to only focus on the first half, we never see the "evidence" that has been backing it up. Once we look at both halves, we often find ourselves delighted to discover how quickly we can punch these reasons full of holes.

Chapter 24

Talk Yourself to Sleep

*"Cats are rather delicate creatures and they are sub-
ject to a good many different ailments, but I have
never heard of one who suffered from insomnia."*
—Joseph Wood Krutch

From time to time people tell me they have trouble falling
asleep. If I determine they are suffering from an overactive
mind, listening to a seemingly endless flow of inner chatter,
I'll guide them through a remarkable little sleep-inducing
exercise.

Without fail, when I ask people to think about the last
time they had trouble falling asleep, and then have them
tune into what their inner voice sounded like, they say it
sounded like a teenage kid on too much caffeine, talking
fast, loud, and in an almost anxious tone.

Here's the interesting part: not only can we bring this part
of our experience (our inner dialogue) into our conscious
awareness but we can also alter the structure of this inner
voice.

When I ask people to imagine what their inner voice
would sound like if they were so incredibly sleepy that they
just couldn't keep their eyes open, most are surprised not
only by how easily they are able to manipulate this inner
voice but also by how quickly they begin to feel sleepy, even
as they sit in my office in the middle of the day.

After instructing them on the importance of first altering

their inner dialogue as they stretch out on their bed at night, I have them begin to imagine the sound of a crackling fireplace just a few feet from the foot of the bed. I suggest that they listen to the fire crackle and pop for at least forty-five to sixty seconds, and then begin to allow an image of orange-, yellow-, and blue-tinged flames dancing in a fireplace to come together in their mind.

At this point, they can both watch and listen to the imaginary fireplace in their bedroom. They can now move to yet another sensory system, imagining the fire warming the bottom of their outstretched feet.

Very few people ever make it all the way through this process before they fall deeply asleep. In fact, after they have been doing this procedure for a week or two, simply hearing their inner voice talking in a sleepy manner, this step alone is often enough to put them down for the count, and many are unable to ever again get to the first step of the fireplace scene.

Of course, the fireplace is just one of an unlimited number of scenarios one could use to involve all of the senses; you could use anything that invokes the thoughts and associations you have found relaxing in the past. But regardless of the scene you use, the key to the effectiveness of this technique can be found in the involvement of the auditory, visual, and kinesthetic or feeling part of the experience.

With just a little practice, you'll find that you can go to sleep just about anywhere, anytime you need to.

Chapter 25

Don't Change Your Mind—Just Turn It Around

"I know you think I'm crazy. I go into a different room, and I actually felt like it takes me to a better place, positive instead of negative."
—Martin Lawrence

If you wanted to build the tallest building in town, you have two basic ways of reaching your goal; you could either measure the tallest building and then build one taller, or you could tear down all of the other buildings, and whatever you build will be the tallest one in town.

Clearly, tearing down all of the other buildings requires far more time and effort than simply building one that's taller than any of the others, but isn't that a good metaphor of what so many people do on a daily basis?

What would happen if every time you started to think about why something won't work, you stopped and asked the question, "What are two good reasons that it *will* work?"

Better yet, you might want to use a method that Connirae Andreas calls "reversing presuppositions." Let's say you were thinking about retiring and opening a flower shop, and each time you thought about it, you said something like, "But I really don't have any experience with running a flower shop, so that wouldn't work!"

Using Connirae's method, you would take the reason it would not work and turn it into a reason it would.

Simply ask, "How might the fact that I don't have any

experience running a flower shop actually be a reason that it *would* work?"

Because this question is so different from the kind most people are used to asking, it will feel a bit strange initially, but if you hang with it, you'll be amazed to find that your brain actually begins supplying reasons, or answers to your question.

You might get an answer like, "Well, since you don't know anything about it, you don't have the bad habits other flower shop owners have acquired. Anything you need to know, you can learn."

So many times in life, it comes down to the kind of questions that we ask; ask good questions, get good answers. Ask great questions, get great answers. Far too many people have mastered the art of asking horrible questions, and as a result . . . you guessed it.

So tell me, why *will* your idea work? Anyone can tell you why it won't; break away from the norm, and discover why it *will*.

Chapter 26

Mesmerized by an Eleven-Year-Old under a Maple Tree

"Jose has been key to our depth at catcher. He has developed a good rapport with our pitching staff."
—Bill Stoneman

How often have you met someone briefly, but something about the interaction left you feeling like you had known that person for years? I'll never forget July 1977; I was putting the sissy bar back on my bike so that I could get back to the ramp I had built in an attempt to pull off a stunt like Evel Knievel, when a kid from school walked up.

Although I knew Tommy, I'd never talked to him before. He was on his way to the little grocery store about a block down the street and noticed me playing in my front yard.

I couldn't tell you exactly what Tommy said that day, but I'll never forget how the conversation made me feel. It was as if I were standing across from a mirror image of myself, and Tommy kept saying the same exact words I would if I was the one talking. Never before, in any of the previous eleven years of my life, could I remember having been so relaxed and at ease with someone. When he finally had to leave to get the lunch meat his mother had sent him to get for lunch, I remember just standing there enjoying the feelings of comfort that were whirling through my mind and body.

Twenty-two years later, I would discover exactly what

had happened that summer afternoon. I discovered that it was possible to duplicate in virtually anyone the effect that Tommy had created for me that day.

What I had experienced that day was the synchronization between Tommy and me, of several aspects of my behavior that were just outside of my conscious awareness. Things like my breathing, the rate and speed of my voice (both externally and internally), my posture, and countless other behavioral factors were being mirrored back to me.

On some level, my brain was saying, "Hey, this feels very familiar. This person is just like me." Familiarity is a very powerful driving force in human beings. We have a propensity to move toward things that are familiar, and usually move away from things that are unfamiliar.

Understand, then, that the level of rapport we have with others is very often the difference that makes the difference. My experience has been that until we have received feedback that others are comfortable with us, we should use our time solely for creating this level of comfort and trust.

By intentionally and systematically learning to employ the mannerisms that my friend Tommy was naturally engaging in that afternoon, we not only create a feeling of openness in others but we also can make the interaction more comfortable and enjoyable for us as well.

A few years ago I discovered something that slices through the muck of learning to establish rapport, and which allows someone to create instantly a level of rapport usually achieved only after years of training.

First, allow your lower jaw to drop down one-half to one inch, so that your jaw is loose and relaxed. Next, look at something in front of you, and while keeping your eyes and head pointed in that direction, shift your attention or awareness into your peripheral vision. Become aware of what's just off to the sides, just below, and just above.

Loosening the jaw assists you in disengaging from your

internal chatter and helps your mind go quiet. Shifting to your peripheral vision stimulates your parasympathetic nervous system. As odd as it may sound, when the parasympathetic nervous system is stimulated, it actually causes you to relax.

Now you're ready to close your eyes and take your awareness to the area that surrounds your heart. Focus on this space in your chest for fifteen to twenty seconds. By now, you will have noticed a tremendous shift and softening in your state of mind and body. While continuing to hold your attention here, think about someone you love and appreciate unconditionally. Just let the feelings of love and gratitude you have about this person flood your entire being.

Hold this feeling as long as you want or have time for, and when you are ready, move to the next step and think about the person you will be working or communicating with while holding on to the feeling of love and appreciation. Do this just before meeting with someone, and the aura that will be vibrating from you will be an undeniable force.

Do I do this with everyone I meet? No. I usually reserve this for family and clients. It's so powerful that I don't want to connect with everyone I meet on that level, and chances are, after you experience its power, you won't either.

Chapter 27

You'd Never Put Up with This from Someone Else

"Self-sabotage is when we say we want something and then go about making sure it doesn't happen."
—Alyce P. Cornyn-Selby

Most adults know the misery that comes from being at war with themselves. For countless reasons, most men and women make it to adulthood with a wide range of disparaging comments they say to themselves each day. Fortunately, it's not necessary to pinpoint what contributed to our adoption of self-defeating statements and inner dialogue.

Examples of such statements are "I just don't deserve to be here," and "I'm not as pretty, handsome, skilled, or liked as the other people in this group." Internal statements like this are only strengthened when we argue with them; it's a vicious circle that spins us round and round on a ride of bitterness and discontent.

Traditional wisdom (by now you know I'm anything but traditional) tells us that the only way to win an argument is simply to refuse to enter into one in the first place. While this may very well work for the conversations in our external world, this strategy strips us of a very powerful skill when dealing with conversations in our internal world.

Dr. Steven Reiss, a psychology professor at the University of Ohio and the author of *Who Am I? The 16 Basic Desires that Motivate Our Actions and Define Our Personalities*, wrote about the power of vengeance when it comes to motivation. Initially, many people wrinkle their noses at the thought of vengeance having a useful purpose, but in fact Dr. Reiss found that vengeance spills over into areas that are commonly accepted as noble. Competition is one such example.

Time and time again, I have observed men and women vehemently reject a derogatory comment from someone else and argue to the ends of the earth that the other person is wrong. Perhaps someone calls them a "worthless, lazy bum!" What happens next is predictable: "Who are you calling 'worthless'? You are too stupid to know anything, let alone making a judgment about me. *You* are the one who's stupid!"

Can you see the difference between how we react to comments from others and those that we generate ourselves? More important, have you caught a glimpse of the power this knowledge holds for self-transformation?

Before I reveal a wonderful little gem, let me say that I don't view any technique, however powerful and effective it may be, as a stand-alone method for change. In fact, my audio program *Revealing Happiness* is a collection of multiple principles and methods of self-transformation. We are far too unique as individuals to think that everyone benefits from the same technique.

In one particular session, a client of mine kept repeating, "I always find myself thinking that I don't deserve to succeed."

I said, "Let me ask you something. Was there anyone in high school whom you just couldn't stand?"

She quickly nodded and acknowledged that there was indeed someone whom she had detested. I had her close her eyes and imagine that this high school foe was standing in front of her, waving her finger in her face, and saying, "You don't deserve to succeed!"

As she did this, I could see her entire physiology shift

into a more confident and aggressive posture.

"Give me a report on what you're thinking and feeling as you imagine this scenario." I said.

My client quickly snapped, "I'm thinking, who do you think you are to tell me what I deserve? I deserve anything I want, and I can create anything I want!"

Amazing isn't it? All it takes to kick our butts into gear is to have someone else try and tell us we can't, or that we don't deserve to. Why in the world don't we use this power of our imagination to put this into action now?

Here are step-by-step instructions:
1. Identify something that you routinely say to yourself that tends to deflate you and with which, more often than not, you find yourself agreeing.
2. Think of someone you have considered annoying, and whose ideas you would reject as nonsense.
3. Imagine this person telling you the same thing you told yourself in step 1.

I have watched people take self-defeating comments they had fought with for years and vaporize them in a matter of days just by employing this method.

Chapter 28

Thinking from a Higher Level

"You can never solve a problem on the level on which it was created."
—Albert Einstein

Albert Einstein once said that "a problem cannot be solved on the same level that it exists." I might add that a poor utilization of logical levels can also take a problem and create thought demons that throw your nervous system into a tizzy.

Logical levels might best be described as "aboutness." Using the ladder metaphor, when you have a thought *about* a previous thought, you have just gone up to the next rung. My definition of a logical level is the first level of thinking that involves aboutness, and that no longer relies solely on raw sensory input.

What is sensory input? If you see a handgun in the middle of your living room floor upon entering your home, sensory input is nothing more than the visual information you register when you first see the gun.

Enter the first logical level; you now think to yourself, *What is this gun doing in my house?* You have now had thoughts *about* the gun.

Jumping to the second logical level, you have the opportunity to categorize the gun. This is where we find a huge discrepancy from one person to the next. From this logical level, someone with a teenage son might think, *That kid's at it again. He's always buying something and leaving it laying around. He's so irresponsible.* Another might think, *Someone has broken into my house and kidnapped my son!* The meanings we could assign to what our senses have detected are only limited by our imagination.

The level of certainty a person has *about* the thoughts from the second logical level is important. The person who thinks, *Cool, John has used his money wisely, and bought something that will hold value, instead of spending it on drugs,* will not be experiencing a problem about what he or she has detected. The same cannot be said of the person who thinks, *My son is thinking of killing himself.* The problem this person will experience will have been initially generated by the thoughts *about* the gun, or what it *means* to that person.

A person who has feelings of certainty about those thoughts will have strengthened and solidified the level-two thoughts and feelings, neurologically speaking.

The number of times we can reflect on something, or the number of logical levels we can ascend regarding some sensory-based event, is unlimited. Therefore, we need to understand that each new or "higher" logical-level thought governs, modifies, and alters all that are below it. This understanding offers tremendous insight into the logical level we might work from when wanting to create a change in ourselves or others.

When I am certain that the gun *means* my son is planning to commit suicide, I allow no other thoughts in at that point, and if someone attempts to persuade me otherwise, I will vehemently defend my position.

If, however, my son's possible suicide plot enters my mind, but my thoughts and feelings on the third logical level are a bit shaky or uncertain, my mind will still entertain other possible explanations, and I'll be less likely to begin acting on any certain thought or explanation until I have investigated the matter more fully. This is the mark of a healthy style of thinking.

How can we break out of this loop when the power of our affirmation is producing unfounded behavior? For this we can rely on paradox. Paradox jams things up and frees our thinking and behaving.

How can we use the structure of paradox then?

Let's look at this example from a particular therapist:

> Therapist: Are you sure of that?
> Client: Yes.
> Therapist: Are you sure you're sure?
> Client: Yes.
> Therapist: Are you sure enough to be unsure?

Notice that after the therapist has asked this question, no matter what answer the client gives him, the client has loosened the grip on the thoughts and beliefs that had been limiting thinking. If the client says, "Yes, I'm sure enough to be unsure," the client has accepted that he or she is somewhat unsure. If the client says, "No, I'm not sure enough to be unsure," the client has expressed doubt and, once again, accepted being somewhat unsure.

Let me ask you: what are you sure enough of to be unsure about? Perhaps there's something that you're not sure enough about to be unsure of. Think deeply on this. I'm sure you'll find it as liberating as I have, or the countless clients I have used this technique with to loosen their thoughts.

Chapter 29

Facing Changes by Changing Faces

"A smile confuses an approaching frown."
—Unknown

You've no doubt heard the phrase "laughing like a hyena," or if you grew up in a rural area in the Midwest like I did, "grinning like a possum." I have to admit, I have absolutely no idea what the emotional state of hyenas or possums might be when they have a grin on their face. But if I were to use what research has shown us over and over again, I would tell you that the hyena and opossum would probably be happier than most other animals.

Try this: Check the status of your face every fifteen minutes for a day to see how often you're smiling. You might be surprised to discover how often you are doing the opposite; many people spend the largest part of their day with some form of scowl that corresponds to a less than happy state of mind and body.

I could cite many studies that show a powerful correlation between our facial expressions and what emotions we are experiencing. But why would I want to do that? You can experience it for yourself . . . right now!

Simply raise the corners of your mouth, allowing a gentle and easy smile to spread across your face, and while this is happening allow this to "soften" your eyes. Now, simply hold this for thirty seconds. The shift that you feel is real; by changing the expression on our face, we are simultaneously altering the biochemistry of our body.

I remember a quote I read years ago: "They do not sing because they are happy, they are happy because they sing." The same can be said of a smile; don't wait until you are happy to smile. Start smiling now, and find out how quickly happiness follows.

Something you might find beneficial is to put a soft and subtle smile on your face, and then, while holding that expression, go ahead and think of some challenge that had been worrying you. I think you'll find that the challenge takes on a different feeling—one that is more conducive to happiness and productivity.

Chapter 30

Have You Gone over Your Threshold?

*"True love is like a pair of socks; you gotta have two,
and they've gotta match."*
—Unknown

Chances are good that at some point in your life you have experienced a sudden realization that you were living your life to someone else's plans; you develop an awareness that more decisions in your life than you care to remember have been determined by someone else.

This realization may come in the context of your career, interactions with extended family or neighbors, or your marriage. One thing is certain: When there is harmony in the relationship, we are comfortable having others weigh in on the decision. And isn't it true that when the relationship is really harmonious, we don't even mind having an occasional decision made for us?

How do we know when the relationship is no longer harmonious? John Gottman, Ph.D., the world's foremost expert on the success or failure of marriages, feels that this harmony exists when we feel respected. Using sophisticated video cameras, Gottman has been able to predict with 91 percent accuracy which couples will be divorced within four to six years by watching them interact on camera, and then, using the findings of world-renowned facial expression scientist Paul Ekman, interpreting the communication between them. Where there is consistent contempt shown by one or both partners, the show is pretty much over.

Much of it has to do with what I call going over threshold. Let's say that from time to time, your computer just shuts down and you have no idea why. Now, if this only happens once every two weeks, you'll probably go a long time before you finally need to buy a new one. Let this same thing start happening once a day, though, and it won't be long before you toss it through the window and head off to buy a new one.

Imagine a glass tube about eight inches in diameter and six feet long resting vertically against a wall in your home. Like a giant thermometer, it has a red liquid that rises when you are upset or angry. Start at a baseline where all of the liquid is pooled at the bottom of the tube. Enter the first experience where your partner makes some cutting remark; the liquid now comes up about two feet in the tube. Given enough time before the next hurtful remark, the liquid will have returned to its starting position.

What about a situation where the liquid has come up two feet and has only gone down halfway before the next sarcastic remark comes your way? Now the red liquid is pushing the three-foot mark. Then, if before the liquid has a chance to go back down, you are angered or hurt again, what happens? This pattern eventually ratchets the red liquid all the way to the top, and then . . . *boom!*

When this happens I call it going over threshold. Once we have gone past our threshold we experience an emotional pop. Just as a bubble that has popped can no longer return to its previous form, neither can most of us ever return to the same feelings we had before the pop.

We often hear this expressed with such phrases as "I just don't feel anything for him anymore," or "It's just not there. It's gone. It's like I'm numb."

Such comments verbally describe the emotional landscape of a person's inner world. Can people hold a relationship together once they hit this point? I think you would agree that people can hold it together even in the bleakest of conditions when they let the fear of the unknown control their destiny.

Chapter 31

Truth or Consequences

"A lie would have no sense unless the truth were felt as dangerous."
—Alfred Adler

Early in the spring of 2008 I had one of the most adrenaline-provoking experiences I'd had in over a decade. I had the opportunity to ride with the Missouri State Highway Patrol doing drug interdiction.

The violations that triggered stops were varied, but in general they were for excessive speed, expired plates, or driving (rather than passing) in the passing lane. This last one was rather informative for me, as I had a habit of driving in that lane just to get a better view of what was ahead—oops. Once the driver of the car that the police had pulled over was seated in the front seat of the patrol car (with me having moved to the backseat), the fun would begin.

The patrolman I was riding with had developed a very successful questioning strategy over the years. It allows him to intuitively know whether he should ask for permission to search a vehicle.

He would begin with simple questions like "Where do you live?" "Where do you work?" "Where are you going?" It wasn't the answer to the initial questions that offered any useful feedback. Whenever they would answer, he would then ask a question about that answer, and then the next, and so on. If the initial answer they gave was designed to throw him off of their real reason for traveling on this day, it would soon become obvious. Each subsequent answer took more processing time, since the driver was having to make up new answers so all related logically to the original answer . . . and that's hard to do.

A typical conversation went something like this:

Patrolman: "Where you going today?"
Driver: "To visit a friend."
Patrolman: "Where does your friend live?"
Driver: "In Lansing, Michigan."
Patrolman: "Really. I'm somewhat familiar with that area. What street does he live on?"
Driver (after a noticeable delay in answering): "On the south side. I can't really remember the exact street address. I just kind of know the landmarks."
Patrolman (asking a critical question): "How long has your friend lived there?"
Driver: "About nine months, now . . . I'm not really sure, maybe a year."
Patrolman: "So what are you guys going to do?"
Driver: "I think we're going to go camping."
Patrolman: "When was the last time you were up there?"
Driver: "It was a couple of years ago."
Patrolman: "Oh, so you have been there before? I mean that's how you know how to get there, with the landmarks and all?"
Driver: "That's right."
Patrolman: "Question: You said he's only lived there nine months to a year, and yet you drove there about two years ago?"
Driver (with a look of obvious confusion and panic setting in): "Why are you asking so many questions?"
Patrolman: "Would it be okay with you if we search

your vehicle?"
Driver: "I'd rather you not. Just give me my ticket so I
can get on my way."

At this point the K-9 officer arrived, and the fun began.

Isn't it true that there have been times in your life that knowing someone was lying would have been helpful? Wouldn't you want to know if your kids were hanging out with a known drug dealer?

Unfortunately, no method I know allows us to read the minds of our children so we can better protect them. We can, however, use our awareness to notice how smoothly they are responding to our questions so we can get a gut feeling about the truthfulness of their answers.

The wonderful part about this approach is that you can use it without seeming like you are an interrogator. Used with the right tone of voice and body language, you can even come across as someone who is genuinely interested. I fully advocate first accessing a state of genuine curiosity, as this step helps generate the necessary nonverbal signals.

Chapter 32

Did He Just Ask Me a Question?

*"One who asks a question is a fool for five minutes;
one who does not ask a question remains a fool
forever."*
—*Chinese proverb*

What in the world does asking questions have to do with
captivating your audience? Everything! Imagine the feeling
of being able to hold the attention of everyone you're speaking to. The fact is, unless you can keep the audience's eyes
and ears riveted, your message is watered down at best.

One of the most powerful uses of language for securing
attention without coming across as pushy is the use of hidden questions. Direct questions can sometimes seem a bit
blunt; we have a tendency to resist someone we feel is trying to probe and inquire too much. Asking questions in a
certain way, however, can bypass the resistance that is often
inherent when asking direct questions.

If, for example, you ask, "How many people here today
have run a red light recently?" you may trigger some nerv-
ousness or resentment among the audience members. By
changing the way you ask that question, they won't even
know you've posed a question. If you say, "Now, I don't
know how many of you have run a red light recently . . . ,"
a very different experience will unfold.

Let's examine what happens when it's "asked" in this
manner. The listeners' minds will access the exact same

thing. Think of it like this: if you ask the question directly, they'll think about whether they have run a light or not. Using the hidden question causes them to think the very same thing, with one *huge* difference: they feel as though *they decided* to think about it when you use the power of hidden questions.

Powerful communicators know how effective questions can be for capturing the attention of others. They also know that sometimes questions, when asked directly, can backfire. Beginning today, insert hidden questions into your conversations and presentations, and watch how much warmer your listeners become.

Chapter 33

Why the Words "Vince Harris" Are the Most Powerful Words in the World

"You can make more friends in two months by becoming interested in other people than you can in two years by trying to get other people interested in you."
—Dale Carnegie

Why are the words "Vince Harris" the most persuasive words in the world to me? All other words fall short of the power of your name for captivating your attention.

While I had always been aware of the effect of calling people by their first name, not until about four years ago did Lanny Masters introduce me to an extreme version of this communication tool.

Lanny had a peculiar but powerful way of using a person's name while telling a story. One day he was going on about a car he used to have, telling me all about the engine, tires, and so on. Now, I normally find talking about cars about as interesting as watching paint dry, but on this particular afternoon I was truly interested in what he was saying and actually learned a great deal.

Lanny elaborated on the massive engine under the hood of his hot rod. "I mashed down on the gas, those tires started spinning, and, Vince Harris, I'm telling you, the power of that car was mind-blowing."

About once every one to two minutes, he would insert

my name, "And Vince Harris . . ." Just hearing my full name every few moments was enough to interest me in something that I normally find painfully boring. Because hearing both our first *and* last name spoken is rare, it makes it stand out that much more.

Do you want to command and keep the attention of others? Begin using their full names as you speak; for me, hearing "Vince Harris" is music to my ears, and I assure you that others will find your use of their full names melodic as well.

Chapter 34

Are They Really Mad, or Are You Really Wrong?

"For it was not into my ear you whispered, but into my heart. It was not my lips you kissed, but my soul."
—Judy Garland

Who has not experienced rage, insecurity, fear, or some other negative emotion just from having a certain look cast our way?

If a waitress gives you a look that just doesn't settle well, it probably won't be a big deal; it may not be comfortable, but it's not like you have to see her every day. However, if this look shows up on a consistent basis from someone you see daily, it might present a challenge. Encounter this look from a spouse or significant other on a regular basis, and you have the makings of what we refer to here in the Midwest as a tussle.

Unfortunately all too often our misinterpretation of others' facial expressions leads to unnecessary turmoil. Odd as it may seem, many people who have been married for years rarely identify correctly the nonverbal messages of their spouse.

The primary reason for misinterpretation is that these messages take place on an unconscious level, just below the threshold that would allow us to make clearer distinctions.

Therapists and counselors who have been divorced are often ridiculed for offering marriage advice to others. But let me share something with you: if you truly want to learn how to enhance your marriage, do not rule out the possibility that someone who has been divorced or who has had a very rocky marriage but then turned things around could provide you with good counsel.

Couples who have always had a stable relationship cannot always tell you how they did it. Why? It's really rather simple. Success can be a great teacher, but it is not always the best teacher.

When things are going well, we rarely stop to question why things are running so smoothly. Those who have turned things around, on the other hand, have been prodded by the pain of their previous condition. They discover and bring into their conscious awareness the patterns of behavior responsible for their strife, affording them the opportunity to tell others precisely what creates the happiness they experience.

Those who are the happiest in their relationships have mastered the skill of reading the face of those they are close to.

John Gottman, the world's foremost researcher on successful marriages, offers the following four keys to consider. Utilizing these keys can enhance your people-reading skills and your ability to empower your relationships with unbelievable levels of unity and bliss:

1. *Identify what the person's face looks like when he or she is in a neutral state.* It's a whole lot easier to distinguish one expression from another when you know what their "clean slate" face looks like.

2. *Realize that people generally experience more than one emotion.* What you observe on the face of another is often a mixture of several emotions at once. If the person is trying to conceal feelings, the process gets even trickier. Therefore, thinking someone is mad, sad, happy, and so on, may only be partially true.

3. *Don't mistake habitual facial features as temporary emotional signals.* Some people naturally have mouths with downturned corners, making them appear unhappy.

4. *Slow down and really look.* Since most emotions are fleeting, and facial expressions at times speed by in a blur, it's important to develop our observational skills over time. When you're uncertain what a look means, ask the person what it means or what he or she is feeling.

You've probably already thought of several instances where you wound up in an argument with someone because the look on his or her face triggered something inside you. Perhaps the memory of an abusive parent or a bully at school was triggered by a similar look on someone's face as you were being taunted. With such mental associations, you'll be needlessly enduring upsets and arguments over and over again.

Enjoy making these discoveries and expanding your awareness of the impact that a simple look from another can have on you. Watch what happens to your relationships!

Chapter 35

Dealing with Reality Once and for All

"Reality is the only word in the English language that should always be used in quotes."
—Unknown

A recent discussion with someone who had gone to several marriage counseling sessions with her husband highlighted one very important fact. This woman talked of the day the counselor asked her husband how he knew that one of his complaints was true. Hesitantly he acknowledged that he didn't know for sure, and he admitted that he had no evidence to support his assertion. However, he continued to say that it was what he thought was the cause of the problem.

Once we are convinced of something, our imagination can run away with us. Whether you are imagining the mailman having a steamy affair with your wife or the sexy little vixen at the cosmetic counter running her fingers through your husband's hair, you are processing it with the very same part of the brain that would be at work if you actually witnessed the real thing.

Don't believe it? Go up to a friend and stand directly in front of him, close enough that you can see the pupils of his eyes. Ask him to imagine he is standing on top of a roof, and suddenly he slips and falls. Watch his eyes. His pupils will constrict and become much smaller momentarily—just like they would if he way really on the roof.

Our nervous system responds just as powerfully to the

pictures and movies in our head as it does to the actual experience.

Jealousy is a very misunderstood emotion. If you actually see your spouse in bed with someone else, that's not jealousy. That's anger. No one on earth would accuse you of being deranged for stringing someone up by her heels at that point. In fact, many people have walked free after murdering their spouse *and* the other man or woman, after unexpectedly walking into a clandestine version of afternoon delight. That's right; even juries recognize that some situations push otherwise normal people over the edge.

So what is jealousy then? In the context we're talking about here, jealousy is when you have never seen anything inappropriate between your spouse and someone else, but you feel insecure, anxious, or angry when your spouse is in the presence of this person. How does that happen? It requires you to be making pictures or movies in your mind about what they could be doing, and then reacting to your personal mind circus. Again, don't believe it? Try this: Grab a small bean bag or something comparable, and then begin tossing it back and forth from one hand to another. As you do so, recite the multiplication tables out loud. If you can access and maintain jealous feelings while doing this, please get in touch with me. The people at the *Guinness Book of World Records* are always looking for neurological anomalies.

The Reality Principle makes it impossible to engage in the nonsense that allows you to get cranked up and jealous. Emotional experiences that are the result of something that comes from the outside world are feelings. Conversely, an emotional experience born out of memory or that which is in our mind is called "prefeeling." You and I, and everyone else in the world, will enjoy life, or not, to the degree that we can keep from mixing these two. The Reality Principle says that whenever you are receiving ample input from the outside world, it will override and dominate input from your inside world.

When does your mind wonder the most? Isn't it when you are on a long drive or when you are tossing and turning in bed? Let me ask you: when was the last time you were driving in heavy traffic during a downpour and experienced jealous feelings? Again, unless you are one of those who will be contacting me for entry into the *Guinness Book of World Records*, it's never happened. In a situation like this, simply too much external input is going on for this mind garbage to have any impact.

Have you ever "known" that if someone would just change his behavior, you would be happy? Or have you ever "known" the reason someone was ignoring you was because she didn't like you, only to discover later that she was just shy?

Start asking, "How do I know for sure?" Then keep asking that question of any answer you come up with. This tactic makes you slow down and notice just how much you really assume in life. If you think your mother doesn't come over for a particular reason, ask! If you are correct, *then* you can address it. However, if you are wrong, think of the resentment you'll create by never taking the time to verify your self-generated motion pictures.

Take seven days and commit to asking, "How do I know?" about anything you "know" that is causing you grief. I think you'll like what you discover.

Chapter 36

The Real Reason That You Don't Belch in Church

"Manners are the hypocrisy of a nation."
—Honore de Balzac

Visionary and pioneer of personal development audio recordings Earl Nightingale once said, "In the absence of a good role model, simply observe what everyone else is doing—and don't do that!" Vernon Howard, author of several powerful books on the power of the human mind/spirit, wrote, "The Truer the Fewer."

My wife and I have a code sound that we utter to each other when we have witnessed someone engaging in flock or herd behavior; we make the *baa* sound. It's a reminder for us to spend less time going with what is popular and to think for ourselves.

Kevin Hogan writes that a large part of how we behave has more to do with what we think the values of those around us are than with our own.

What have you avoided, not because it violated your values, but because you were afraid it might violate someone else's?

Many people fall into the trap of thinking they are following their own path when all they are really doing is polarizing *against* something. I was the poster child for this vicious cycle from my teens through much of my twenties. I shudder to think about the number of things I did for no other reason than to *not* do what someone told me I should do.

It's important to develop an awareness of the distinction between doing what you really want and doing something only to *not* do what someone else wants. The first generally leads to feelings of freedom and pleasure; the second causes you to resent not only others but yourself as well.

Here's the test:

Ask yourself, "If I was suddenly the only person left alive and could do anything I wanted to, would I still choose this path?"

Suppose you want to do something, but you are afraid that someone else in your life might not approve. The question is, "If I knew that so-and-so approved or did it themselves, would I do so without hesitation?"

I once heard a well-known speaker tell a story about one of his friends realizing at the age of thirteen that she had been following the herd. His friend told of how she had always eaten her hamburger with ketchup only. One day she thought, *Whose hamburger is this?* She was eating her hamburger exactly like her mother always did. Because of her close relationship with her mother, she was unconsciously eating so as not to offend her mother.

I remember one time I had only nine hundred dollars, a borrowed car, and a cheesy apartment to my name. I took seven hundred of my nine hundred dollars and flew to San Juan, Puerto Rico, for a week. I'll never forget being told of my father's comments: "I don't know what he's thinking. He can't afford to go to Puerto Rico." My only thoughts were, *I must have been able to, because I did.*

I still think back on that trip as a relaxing, mind-freeing experience that I'll never forget. From a strictly financial perspective it didn't make sense. But let me suggest to you that making your decisions from purely financial perspectives is a sure way to find yourself on your deathbed with a ton of regret. The time I spent on the oncology floor at the San Diego Naval Hospital, holding the hands of people in their last hours here on earth, taught me that people regret all the things they didn't do in life. The trips they *never* took, the things they *didn't* say, the hobbies they *didn't* pursue, the things they thought about doing—but *didn't*.

If someone approached me today and offered me twenty-five thousand dollars to strip my mind of the memory of that trip to Puerto Rico, I'd say, "No, thank you!" Experiences are yours forever.

Chapter 37

Why Time Goes Faster Each Year

"The secret of life is to enjoy the passage of time."
—James Taylor

Have you ever wondered why time seems to go by so much faster each year? Remember when you were a kid coming home from your last day of school before summer break? Isn't it true that the summers seemed to last forever? And do you remember how long the school year lasted in grade school? What about now? Don't you find that summers now seem to go by in a blur?

When you were ten years old, one year represented one-tenth, or 10 percent, of your entire life. When you are fifty years old that same year represents only one-fiftieth, or 2 percent, of your life. As a result, a year seems only one-fifth as long as it did at age ten. What does this mean if we apply this formula to various periods of our life?

When you were six years old, a year seemed like three years; thus, a nine-week summer vacation seemed like twenty-seven weeks! How many times have you heard someone say that life starts after forty, fifty, or sixty-five? At the age of sixty-five you have only 5 percent of your life left in terms of how you will experience time!

I watched my father trudge off to work at 4:30 a.m. each day, coming home at 3:30 p.m. angry, upset, and frustrated by a job he hated. I do not remember ever hearing my father say anything good about his job, ever. My father endured nearly forty years at a place of work he hated so he could provide for his family and then relax for the last 5 to 7 percent of his perceptual life.

I offer this suggestion for the coming year: *Stop* thinking about the things you can do when you retire. Make the decision today that if you are not currently doing something you enjoy, you will be by the end of the year.

Time *does* seem to go faster as we grow older, and will continue to do so at the rate described above. We don't have nearly as much time as we think. So what would you do if you knew you only had five years left to live? Two years? One? Would you do *anything* differently? Whatever your answer, what's stopping you from doing it *now*?

It's been suggested that there are two kinds of people: those who make plans and those who make excuses. My intuition is that you are more interested in making plans. Otherwise, you'd be doing something constructive, like playing video games, instead of reading this book.

I am proposing to you that when you *do something you enjoy for a living*, in a sense you are already enjoying retirement. However, I'm willing to bet at that point the idea of retirement probably won't even enter your mind. Why would it? No one looks forward to the day they can stop doing something they enjoy!

Chapter 38

Better Not Use *That* Finger

"At some point in time, he made a hand gesture in the direction of the officer with what was believed to be a weapon."
—Ricky Boren

As a professional speaker, part of my job is to create and maintain an atmosphere of receptivity in the audience members. One would think that the most powerful tool at the disposal of professional speakers would be the words they choose—and words are important—but one tool in particular is far more powerful.

See, the words are generally what people are most conscious of and what they are paying the most attention to, which is one of many reasons that body language is so incredibly influential. So much is going on nonverbally that it's simply too much for people to track consciously, yet their unconscious mind is paying very close attention to everything.

When was the last time that your eyes slammed shut and your head twisted to the side or jerked backward, only to determine a second later that a bug was about to fly into your eye? This is but one example of the way in which the unconscious mind monitors everything around you.

We've all had the experience of meeting someone and almost instantly getting a bad vibe, just as many of us have met someone who minutes later felt like an old friend. What on earth can we know about people seconds or minutes after meeting them? Very little. But sometimes that proves to be more than enough.

Let's examine one particular aspect of body language: the gesture of pointing with the index finger. While using this gesture may empower speakers and make *them* feel confident, it's one of the quickest ways I know to generate negative feelings in others. In fact, in one particular experiment, 72 percent of the participants rated a speaker using a finger point as negative, finding the person aggressive and rude. Furthermore, these same participants were not able to recall nearly as much of the presentation as those in the group listening to the speaker when he gave the same presentation without pointing.

Clearly, using your hands to gesture allows you to communicate more powerfully. Just try giving a presentation with your hands tied and see what happens to your effectiveness as a communicator. So, if pointing with the index finger is a bad idea, how can we punctuate with our hands, making a segment of our message stand out?

Just touch the tip of your index finger and the tip of your thumb together, while leaving the rest of your hand open and relaxed. Anytime you might have used your index finger to point in the past, simply substitute it with this gesture.

When audience members in the aforementioned experiment were asked to evaluate speakers who touched their thumb and index fingertips together, they rated the speaker as focused and thoughtful.

If you would like to incorporate this gesture into your communication, the best thing to do is get in front of a mirror. Play with this new gesture, discovering just how many ways you can use it to eloquently embellish your message.

The faster you get comfortable using this gesture, instead of the archaic finger point, the faster you'll find others becoming pleasantly receptive to both you and your message.

Chapter 39

The Painfully Happy Way of Getting Things Done

"People often say that motivation doesn't last.
Well, neither does bathing—that's why we
recommend it daily."
—Zig Ziglar

Millions of magazines are sold each month simply because of a few words on the cover. The words "Weight Loss Secrets," or something similar, compel people to buy a magazine. They are looking for an easy way to lose weight and keep it off. They are dissatisfied with the way they look or feel, but not necessarily with the process or behaviors that are responsible for how they look and feel. Namely, they do not dislike eating or sitting on their butt instead of exercising.

For most people, the relief they experience comes from *not* doing the behaviors that will help. When they choose to watch TV instead of going to the gym, or to eat three slices of cake instead of one, they feel a welcome comfort . . . for a little while.

Have you ever known people who ignored their health for thirty, forty, or fifty years, eating what they want, never exercising or getting an annual physical? My guess is that you've also known people who, after a near-fatal heart attack, got back on their feet and completely changed their life. They exercise every day, eat only healthy foods, and visit their doctor regularly. What happened?

Pain is an incredible tool for getting someone to take immediate action. It's been said that everyone has a breaking point, and my experience is that this breaking point comes when we have hit our pain threshold.

Studies have shown that when overweight men and women read an article that talks about the tragic events that can result from remaining overweight, their eyes skip across that section, and they begin reading again where the text shifts to another, less painful, topic.

Here's the secret to weight loss:

Exercise seven days a week, at least thirty minutes a day, with enough intensity to break a sweat; eat healthier foods; and consume fewer calories.

And here's the secret to making that happen:

Dip your heart, mind, body, and soul into the pain you will experience if you don't.

I don't mean read about it. I mean close your eyes and imagine your loved ones sobbing uncontrollably at your funeral. When *you* are crying, you will have taken the first step in getting the leverage to change your life for the long haul.

The movie *The Secret* is very effective at giving the viewer a good warm feeling and a sense of gratification. However, the idea of the Law of Attraction has, in some cases, created more confusion and turmoil than anything else. If you are seventy pounds overweight and you have high blood pressure and Type II Diabetes, feeling warm and having a sense of gratification is going to take you to an early grave. If you *do* want to live a longer and healthier life, however, thinking about being thinner and feeling good about it is not going to attract anything other than denial about your current situation.

Sadly, *The Secret* has spurred many people into thinking that negative or painful thoughts are forbidden and are to be pushed away like the plague. To do so, though, is to leave behind the most powerful motivator on earth: *pain*.

Kevin Hogan has brought to public awareness what I consider to be one of the most valuable visualization methods for using pain constructively. It involves split-screen imaging and is based on recent research on visualization and motivation.

Imagine for a moment that in front of you is a 60-inch television. Imagine a line splitting the screen vertically; on the left side is an image of how you look now and examples of all of the bad or painful things you can expect if you stay this way. On the right side is an image of you looking how you would look at your desired weight. With that image, be sure to place all of the benefits of looking and feeling like that "you." The key is to observe them both at the same time.

Why does this work so powerfully? Two words: *cognitive dissonance*. Your brain and nervous system freak when two contrasting images or thoughts are held simultaneously. It is simply too uncomfortable, and therefore your unconscious has one primary goal at this point: resolve the pain. If the image on your left side is painful enough, your brain will do whatever it has to do to bring your reality into alignment with the healthy image on the right side. What will have to happen? You guessed it: exercise and changing eating habits.

Pain is not a negative or positive thing. It is simply a tool that is appropriate at times, and not so appropriate at others.

Chapter 40

High Self-Esteem or Idiot?

"The truest characters of ignorance are vanity, pride, and arrogance."
—Samuel Butler

How can you tell if people have high self-esteem? Watch how they treat those from whom they need nothing. How do they treat the waitress, the gas station attendant, or the bellhop?

We are often tricked into thinking that the person with a big ego has high self-esteem. This isn't the case, though. In fact, having a big ego and high self-esteem at the same time is impossible. Let's look at two different scenarios:

A. The person without much ego and low self-esteem
B. The person with a big ego and low self-esteem

The person lacking much ego and having low self-esteem is likely to take the negative things that happen in life and direct them inward, blaming himself or herself. People with a big ego and low self-esteem, however, are more likely to blame others and project frustration and anger outward. In other words, the things that go wrong in their life will always be someone else's fault.

The more accepting we are of ourselves, the more accepting we are of others. It's hard, bordering on impossible, to be any more accepting of others than we are of ourselves.

Many people confuse moods with self-esteem. Moods are very temporary, and they serve as a filter through which we view the world at that moment. People with very high self-esteem don't have nearly as much sway in their behavior when they experience changing moods.

On the other hand, those with low self-esteem are more or less driven by their ever-changing moods. In short, the quality of the life they experience is all wrapped up in their moods.

There may be times when people don't feel like doing a task they had promised they would do. People with low self-esteem let the mood of "not feeling like it right now" justify not completing the task. Meanwhile, a person with high self-esteem will do it anyway. The message is short, but so powerful: to make lasting changes in your external world, it is essential to build strong self-esteem.

What's one big contribution you can make in this area? The key is to accept yourself as you are right now. As strange as it seems, the longer you reject the things you don't like about yourself, the longer they will persist. The instant you accept the things you have not liked about yourself, they start melting away. If you find yourself thinking that the information in this chapter contradicts the information in the last chapter, use this as an opportunity to begin thinking in terms of this *and* that, instead of this *or* that.

Chapter 41

Travels through the State of Confusion

"Advertising is 85 percent confusion and 15 percent commission."
—Fred Allen

In the age of instant communication, many of us have found ourselves being jerked around like puppets on a string. We respond to every ringing phone, instant message, and just about every other form of the "stop whatever you are doing and talk to me now" demands that come our way.

The result is predictable: a day filled with the stop-start-stop-start pattern that leaves you vulnerable to what Zig Ziglar has often referred to as confusing activity with accomplishment.

Anytime we are moving through the day in a scattered manner, it almost always comes down to the fact that we are not clear about our priorities. If people would stop several times a day and ask themselves, *Why am I doing this?* they'd find that often it was just so they would *not* have to be doing something else.

Think about it: how many times each year after January 1 have you done something like clean the garage to avoid having to do your taxes? Normally, cleaning the garage wouldn't bring much pleasure. However, when contrasted with a tax day, it suddenly becomes an enjoyable endeavor.

So, establishing your priorities for the day is the first step. Only after you have determined what *is* important can you gain an awareness of what *isn't*.

On April 7, 2008, I was having breakfast with my mother. I forgot to turn off my cell phone, and my receptionist sent a text to my phone. When I picked up my phone to turn it off, I could see that I had missed a call from a producer at Fox News. She was calling to see if I was available for a live interview on national television at 3:30 p.m.

You might be thinking, *Vince, did you drop everything and call her back?* No, I didn't. The time I had scheduled with my mother still had about fifteen minutes remaining. In the fifteen minutes I had waited, Kim had found someone else to do the interview.

In terms of publicity, possible speaking engagements, and product sales, a few minutes of airtime on Fox News is worth quite a lot. My mother was sixty-three years old at that time. The day will come when I would trade everything I have for another fifteen minutes with her. I'll take it now instead.

I can't begin to tell you how freeing it was to hire someone to take all of my incoming business calls. If you are answering your own calls, I'll bet a dollar to a doughnut that you are neglecting an important area of your life.

Determine what your priorities for the next day will be. Once you have started working on one, refuse to be distracted by anything less than a true emergency until you are through. I once heard someone suggest that you can only say no and smile when you have a much bigger yes burning inside.

Chapter 42

Exploit Your Strengths and Ignore Your Weaknesses

"Strength does not come from physical capacity. It comes from indomitable will."
—Mahatma Gandhi

I have to admit that I was caught up in the fix-my-weaknesses mind-set at one time. Sound logical? While your weaknesses certainly have to be addressed if they are significant enough, far too often that's just not the case. More often than not, what's really holding people back has more to do with them not focusing on their strengths; they are not maximizing the power they already have and focusing on bringing the weaker aspects of themselves up to par.

I am an idiot when it comes to mechanical things. When my bathtub is leaking I call a plumber. If the computer starts getting goofy I call a computer tech. You get the picture.

My strengths are in presenting, training, teaching, and consulting—all things that involve speaking and talking to other people. Have you ever met someone who was determined to be good at everything? Determined as they may be, one factor makes this an ill-formed goal: *time.*

The one thing we all have the same amount of, whether it's Bill Gates or a homeless person, is the amount of time we have available. We each have twenty-four hours each day. We either use it wisely or we don't.

With very few exceptions, people who are living a life

they always dreamed of did so by setting forth a goal and then focusing most of their time and energy there. They have mastered the use of the Pareto Principle, or the 80/20 Rule. This rule states that 80 percent of the results you create come from just 20 percent of the activities you do.

While it may vary a bit (90/10, 70/30), it's pretty darn close with just about anything you apply it to. Eighty percent of the world's wealth is owned by 20 percent of the people. Eighty percent of the crime is committed by 20 percent of the criminals. Eight percent of any stock portfolio's profits come from 20 percent of the stocks.

Key Point: Since 80 percent of your results come from 20 percent of the things you do, find out what those things are, and do *more* of those and *less* of everything else. The things that you feel like you aren't very good at are probably not part of the 20 percent of the things you do that account for 80 percent of the results. Therefore, in the grand scheme of things they really don't matter that much.

I no longer feel uncomfortable about the areas where I don't excel. Why would I want to take time away from the things I enjoy doing when someone else can do what I need done in a fraction of the time?

If you dedicate the time to identify what you are good at and focus more of your time in that area, the results will be so significant that you'll see your weaknesses for what they are.

Does that mean you have to quit trying to become stronger in your weaker areas? Of course not. Just be sure you are spending most of your time on the 20 percent that accounts for 80 percent of your results.

Chapter 43

Did Earl Nightingale Know about the RAS?

"The most important thing about goals is having one."
—Albert F. Geoffrey

It's hard to make it past the age of ten without having someone tell you about the importance of having goals. I'm always amazed at the number of people who are pushing forward with all of their strength and yet coming up empty-handed.

Whether I'm presenting in New York, Michigan, or North Carolina, one of the most common challenges I hear about comes from not having a crystal-clear goal.

In short, show me someone with a vivid description of what she wants to be experiencing one year, two years, or five years from now—such that it has become hard to not think about it—and I'll show you someone who will bypass those goals with even more education, money, talent, looks, or friends in high places.

Many years ago, Earl Nightingale spoke about this phenomenon in his classic recording *The Strangest Secret.*

What was this strange secret?

We become what we think about most often.

To avoid getting into a weeklong discussion of neurology, I'll simply tell you about the Reticular Activating System (RAS). RAS is the neurological structure which serves as a filter that makes some things nearly impossible to ignore, and blocks other things from ever reaching your conscious awareness.

Remember the last time you bought a new vehicle? Didn't you immediately start seeing similar vehicles everywhere? This had nothing to do with the number of them on the road; they had always been there. Now that *you* have this vehicle, it has suddenly become relevant to you, which causes your RAS to change its filters. It now searches for, and highlights, any match it finds, thrusting its discovery into your consciousness. It happens with clothes, cars, glasses, hairstyles—you name it.

A clearly written goal has the power to turn your RAS on high. Your RAS will allow you to notice the elements of your experience that will enable you to achieve any goal on earth.

The moment you put a pen to paper and start crafting your goal, you begin tweaking your RAS. You change what it detects and what it deletes by determining what is important to you and what isn't. Wanting something is not enough. Until you have written it out in detail, you will not be able to provide your brain with enough information to turn your RAS on full-force.

As you imagine having achieved your goal, what does the outcome look like? Sound like? Smell like? Feel like? Taste like? Describe your goal in such detail that its initial ambiguity turns into a crystal-clear picture.

When you write down your goals this clearly, you better hang on, because your life will rapidly move in that direction.

Chapter 44

Using the Brain of a Waiter to Get Ahead

"Happiness? That's nothing more than health and a poor memory."
—Albert Schweitzer

Have you ever had the experience of having the day off, a chance to unwind and relax, and yet your mind was gnawing at you the whole time?

One reason for this is that most people have a great deal of unfinished business hanging around. If you have ever started something, but then had to place it on the back burner and move on to something else, then you know exactly what I'm talking about.

Back burner or not, the "out of sight, out of mind" theory does not hold water here. When a task is not complete, it will amplify the feelings of stress and tension you feel as you move through the day doing other things.

Russian psychologist Bluma Zeigarnik made a discovery that explains why this occurs. He noticed that waiters remembered in great detail the orders that were pending—the ones that had not yet been served.

However, as soon as they had placed the meal on the table, the waiters immediately forgot what had been ordered. What has now been termed as the Zeigarnik Effect explains why unfinished business can literally wear us down, sending us into overwhelm.

The Zeigarnik Effect creates a psychic tension to drive us

to complete an action. Once the waiter had placed the plate on the table, it was a finished project, and the mind discharged that information as it was no longer relevant. This "release" cleared conscious space for other things.

What is vitally important to remember, however, is that we only have so many chunks of conscious space available. When we overload consciousness, we begin to feel stressed and confused.

Many physical manifestations of illness may also be the result of unfinished business. Certain emotional or psychological experiences that were not effectively dealt with at the time can cause problems long after the event has passed.

Cardiologists often refer to what is known as the Anniversary Effect—the tendency for people to return on or around the anniversary date of a traumatic experience. In order to restore and maintain balance, we must increase our capacity for health.

As we start to close loops by finishing old business, we start to see our health making positive turns. This may involve working through the list of actual projects we have opened, that are *still* open, far longer than they should have been, or effectively dealing with the psychological junk from something that was not handled adequately at the time.

While we cannot change the past, we can change the manner in which we have been responding—consciously, unconsciously, or both—to a particular event.

Chapter 45

Are You Doing the Right Things, or Just Doing Things Right?

"People, like nails, lose their effectiveness when they lose direction and begin to bend."
—Walter Savage Landor

Successful people do things that unsuccessful people refuse to do. Successful people generally don't like doing them either, but their dislike is subordinated by their strength of purpose. Successful people have the ability to focus on doing the *right things*, which makes all the difference in the world.

Clients often tell me about their lack of time and how stressed their life is because they just can't get things wrapped up. I always listen closely to what follows. After they are through talking business, and they start to chitchat about life in general, I almost always hear the self-imposed obstacles to their progress.

When someone can tell me about the personal life of the contestants on *American Idol*, or give me the play-by-play scoop on last night's baseball game, I know I have someone before me who cannot see the forest for the trees. My company commander in boot camp had one standard reply when someone used the "I didn't have time" excuse. He would simply ask, "Did you sleep last night?" Of course, the answer was always "yes." He would scream, "Then you had time!"

The sad fact is that most people simply are not willing to pay the price for the things they say they want. We all have to either pay the price of discipline or the pain of regret.

The things that will really count toward the achievement of your goals are most likely at odds with the way the rest of the world lives. When you begin to use a part of each of your days off to work on things that will help you achieve one or more of your goals, many people just won't get it. Most people hate their jobs so much that all they can think about is anything *except* work-related activities. If this is your situation, let that be the first indication that you are not following your heart.

One of my early mentors explained to me that if a person would read ten minutes a day on one particular topic, then in five years that person would be in the top 2 percent of experts in that field. I took that to heart, but I cheated a little. I decided to read at least an hour each day, and as a result I am an expert in each of the subjects I write about and teach.

I became a recluse of sorts. I chose to spend my time alone doing productive things, only venturing out to mingle with others whom I felt had a positive direction in their lives. As you might imagine, that limited the number of people I had to hang out with, but that decision changed my life.

If you have been frequently saying, "I just don't have enough time to exercise, read, or write," the real problem is not a lack of time, but a lack of clearly defined priorities. In other words, you are probably spending a great deal of time doing things that you enjoy, rather than the things that matter.

Before you complain about not having enough time to do the things that matter the most, first take a look at how much time you are wasting doing things that provide escape but do not move you to the next level.

Chapter 46

What Does Your Life Mean?

"Your life's meaning is the difference that it makes. If it doesn't make a difference, it has no meaning."
—Lyndon Duke

Lyndon Duke is best known for his studies on the linguistics of suicide. Duke felt that if you could understand suicide, you would also develop an understanding for all human unhappiness.

He once suggested that when we are on our deathbed, we will be asking, "What is different on this planet because I was here?" If nothing is different, then you didn't make a difference. If you didn't make a difference, then your life had no meaning.

Lyndon had experienced exceptional success early in his life. Later, after a series of events, he had hit rock bottom. One day, as he lay face down on his living room floor, he heard his neighbor mowing the yard. Along with the sound of the lawn mower, he also heard his neighbor singing as he mowed.

In a flash, Duke realized what he wanted more than anything else. He wanted to experience a life so simple that he could mow the yard and sing at the same time. His new goal was to simply become an average person. He came to the understanding that one's life did not have to be exceptional, and that an average person, living an average life every day, could make a big difference.

Remember, Duke defined meaning as the difference that you make. Lyndon Duke made the differences he was able to make, and didn't get frustrated about the differences he couldn't.

Duke knew something that many never figure out: We find the things we do frequently easier to do, which includes accessing emotions like misery and frustration. If we practice being miserable and frustrated, we become more proficient at being miserable and frustrated.

By studying those who had taken their own life, and looking at what he called the linguistics of suicide (studying their suicide notes), Duke discovered that many people who had taken their own lives had the unrealistic expectation that every moment of every day had to be the most spectacular ever. If it wasn't, something was wrong. These people navigated their way through life with a rigid set of rules about what constitutes a good day. These rules made having a good day all but impossible.

Many of the things you would rather not experience in your life will happen. People you love will die or get sick. Things will break. Earthquakes, floods, hurricanes, and tornados will continue to claim innocent lives. When you accept this fact ahead of time, your ability to bounce back is enhanced tremendously.

What would it be like for you to experience a series of happy average days? The next time you are convinced that you are having a terrible day, ask yourself what would have to happen for you to call it a fun or successful day. Make it easier to have great days and more difficult to have bad ones. Most people have it set up the other way around!

Chapter 47

The Cocktail Party Factor

"Insecurity is just something that's there all the time.
I've never been crippled by it."
—Catherine Keener

I'll never forget my experience with a woman who had booked an appointment with me after telling me she had "no self-esteem." After I had asked her a few questions she firmly stated, "I *know* I have no self-esteem, because every time I walk into a room, I just know that everyone is talking about me!"

"Wow, that's really arrogant and self-centered," I quipped. "Mary, have you ever considered that maybe everyone else is so busy worrying that people are talking about them that they don't have time to think about you?" I asked. "Most people who walk into a room are convinced that everyone else is focusing exclusively on them. If this does happen, they are only focusing on us long enough to worry about what we might be thinking about them." Then I gave Mary an exercise designed get her out of her own head and shift her attention to the outside world.

I had her close her eyes and pretend that as she walked into a room, she could see the thoughts people were having in a cartoon bubble above their heads, containing such words as "They probably know this jewelry isn't real" or "I think she can tell I've had a hair transplant."

A few weeks later, she reported back to me that while it

had been great fun at first, she later had simply gone about the business of thinking about her own purpose for entering a room of people. If she had gone in to make a new friend, then that's what she did. If she had gone in to obtain some information for her latest venture, then that's what she did.

No longer was she wasting valuable time fretting about what others might be thinking of her. And on the rare occasion that she started to worry, she'd instantly zero in on the thought bubbles of others, and find herself giggling inside seconds later.

How much more would you accomplish if you didn't let the imaginings of what others might think crop up during the creative stages of your project?

Unfettered thinking can, and does, lead to insightful breakthroughs and advances. Some people once believed that the idea of a man walking on the moon was lunacy. I'm sure Neil Armstrong is glad that NASA didn't concern itself with what these naysayers thought.

How many projects have you finished, knowing in your heart that you had much better "stuff" buried inside, "stuff" that you chose to leave buried because of how silly someone might find your ideas? Resolve to stop doing this now, and start expressing your strengths. You can always edit later. But first, just get it out!

Key Point: Realize that your thoughts about what others might think act as a vise that clamps down on your stream of creativity. Understand that no one is thinking about you as much as you think, and if they are, this only serves as proof that they are insecure and not as relevant as you might have previously thought.

Chapter 48

Be a "Pen" Head and Choose Your Friends Wisely

"The tartness of his face sours ripe grapes."
—William Shakespeare

Let me give you a quick example of how rapidly and easily you can change what you're feeling by simply making some changes in what you do with your face.

Place a pen or a pencil in your mouth, holding it on each end with your fingers, keeping it horizontal to your face. Push it as far back between your upper and lower teeth as you can so that it pulls the corners of your mouth tight. Then, just bite down slightly to hold it there. Hold it there for thirty to sixty seconds. As strange as it may seem, you will most likely start to feel a positive emotional shift.

Now, take this pen or pencil, and trap it between your nose and your upper lip, by scrunching up your top lip so you can hold it against the bottom of your nose. Hold it there for thirty seconds. You'll be blown away by how fast the good feelings start to reverse.

Mother Teresa believed that peace begins with a smile. After you experience the contrast in feelings between these two exercises, you may find yourself believing it, too. Learning to smile consistently makes everything you do more pleasurable.

Smiling increases pain-killing endorphins and immune system boosters like T-cells. It lowers the stress hormones cortisol, adrenaline, and noradrenaline, and produces hormones that stabilize and even lower blood pressure. Frowning, on the other hand, increases blood pressure, weakens the immune system, and fuels depression and anxiety.

Research has shown that even a fake smile can trick the brain into triggering changes in your biochemistry at lower levels.

You see, simple changes in facial expressions bring about profound changes in the emotions that we are experiencing, which in turn sculpts the moods we operate from most consistently. On top of that, our expressions communicate powerfully to others—so powerfully, in fact, that others may even begin to feel what we are feeling. That *can* be very useful. However, unless you are using this methodically and with intention, you may be inviting them to experience feelings other than those that would be most beneficial.

When I was about seventeen years old, I was standing in a parking lot one night talking with some friends. There was a girl present whom I had seen around before, but I had never spoken to her. I decided to talk to her, and we were talking for a little while before she suddenly stated, "I always thought you were a real jerk, but you're actually a really nice guy!"

I was speechless. I had never spoken to this girl before in my life. How could she have thought I was a jerk when she didn't even know me?

When I was a teenager I had a reputation of being a tough guy. As poor as my self-esteem had been, it felt pretty good to be recognized, even if it was for winning a fight. The more in love I fell with the recognition, the more desperate I became to keep the right to be viewed as a tough guy. What I didn't know, however, was that not everyone perceived my communication the same way.

Back to the girl in the parking lot. When she would see me, she would just get a bad feeling about me. For her, this feeling translated into "He's a jerk!" Years later, I asked her to describe what she felt when she would see me before she got to know me. She said, "I'd see you and feel tense and aggressive, and I just didn't like that feeling."

Why did my aggressiveness make her feel aggressive? One likely explanation is something called a mirror neuron. Mirror neurons cause us to mimic, and thus experience, much of what we observe. These neurons mirror the behavior of the person we are observing, causing our physiology to experience that which we are watching. In 1992, an Italian scientist named Giacomo Rizzolatti was studying the brains of the macaque, a certain species of monkey. While watching the premotor area of the brain, Rizzolatti and his associates observed something interesting. Not only did this area of the monkey's brain light up when the monkey was reaching for an object, it also lit up when watching another monkey or even one of the researchers reaching for an object. The macaque's brain had mentally imitated the very same gesture.

Keep that in mind when you are choosing your associates. Do the people you spend time with behave the way you want to? I don't think I can overemphasize the importance of this point. Use this awareness to bring people into your life who can help you get to the next level.

Chapter 49

Donny and Marie and a Big Round of Applause

"Laughter is higher than all pain."
—Elbert Hubbard

I'll never forget the first time I discovered that not every-thing is what it looks like on the surface, or in this case, what it sounds like.

In 1978 my parents sent me to a track and field summer camp at Brigham Young University in Utah. I stayed with some family friends who had lived right across the street from us in Trenton before moving to Provo, Utah. Bob and Dee Johnson didn't have kids of their own, so they "adopted" me, treating me like the son they had never had. After mov-ing to Utah, Bob had taken a job as the assistant coach for the BYU baseball team, and Dee had taken a position with Osmond Studios. This was at the height of the *Donny and Marie Show*'s popularity, so when I got the chance to go with Dee for a behind-the-scenes tour of Osmond Studios at twelve years old, you can imagine my level of excitement!

While at the studio, I was walking through the audience seating area and noticed signs that lit up to read "Applause" and "Laugh." I couldn't believe it. I looked at the tour guide and asked, "You tell the people when to laugh and when to clap?" I wondered why they didn't just let the people laugh if they thought it was funny.

I didn't know it at the time, but the laughter I heard on some of my favorite TV shows (*The Andy Griffith Show*,

Gilligan's Island, and *Leave It to Beaver*) didn't come from people in a live audience. The laughter I was hearing came from prerecorded laugh tracks. Why did the producers insert these laugh tracks? The television producers knew that when we hear laughter we are more likely to laugh and will actually think something is funnier. I've watched some of my favorite shows without the laugh tracks, and they just aren't as funny.

How can you structure your day so that you can spend more time laughing? What situations could you lighten up a bit by adding a background of humor? Start adding laugh tracks to your life, and see what happens.

Chapter 50

The Reason Mona Lisa Smiles

"Before you put on a frown, make absolutely sure
there are no smiles available."
—Jim Beggs

While laughing triggers a cascade of useful physiological and chemical responses, laughter also contracts the same muscles in our face as a genuine smile. And as you know, putting a smile on our face is very beneficial.

I want to share something with you I learned while in Thailand in the early 1990s—something called the Inner Smile. Relax your face and simply let a very subtle, almost "Mona Lisa"–like smile ease onto your face; just hold that for a bit. Enjoy the sense of ease and comfort that quickly starts flooding your body. Now shift your face into a scowl or frown, and notice the shift in how you feel and your energy level.

Wouldn't it be a shame to have a million dollars in the bank but no way to get it out? I might suggest that it's even worse to have a brain that can release such powerful feelings of happiness and never to smile. A smile is to happiness what a checkbook is to a million dollars in the bank.

Does it seem like we've already talked about this? If you see something more than once, allow that to be a signal of how important it is to your productivity.

Chapter 51

Voted Most Likely to Be Happy

"Success is getting what you want. Happiness is wanting what you get."
—Dale Carnegie

Funny man of the silent movies, Charlie Chaplin, once said, "Life is a tragedy when viewed up close and a comedy in the long shot." Chaplin was reflecting on the power of getting some emotional distance on things perceived as problems. What role does a smile have in creating this emotional distance? Don't we have to be happy before we smile?

I saw a sign in a doctor's office waiting room that read, "They do not sing because they are happy, they are happy because they sing." The same can be said of a smile: "They are not smiling because they are happy, they are happy because they are smiling."

Dr. Dacher Keltner of the University of California has been studying college yearbook photos for over forty years. What he's discovered is just one more reason to start smiling more each day. Dr. Keltner found that those who had the biggest and most genuine smiles in their yearbook photos were, on average, much happier in the years after graduating than those who weren't smiling. What do I mean by "genuine smile"? Over a hundred years ago, Duchenne de Boulogne, a neurologist from France, identified the muscles in our face that contract with a spontaneous happy and genuine smile. In short, a smile that is born from real heartfelt emotions includes the contraction of muscles around the eyes called *orbicularis oculi*. Paul Ekman's research confirmed Duchenne's previous claim that most people could not voluntarily contract this muscle.

That's why we can so easily tell a fake smile. In a forced or fake smile, the contraction of the *orbicularis oculi* remains inactive, and the smile appears less than genuine.

How do we create a genuine smile? When you vividly recall a pleasant or joyous experience, so much so that you once again experience the good feelings that go with the memory, the genuine smile occurs spontaneously. When I remember rocking my daughter to sleep, I don't have to try and smile; when I deeply access this memory, it's just there.

Take a few moments today, and scan through your past for one or two memories that you can instantly use to create the kind of feelings that would generate a beautiful yearbook photo.

Chapter 52

A Different Kind of Body Language

"The illiterate of the future are not those that cannot read or write. They are those that cannot learn, unlearn, relearn."
—Alvin Toffler

Thomas Hanna was the founder of the field of somatics and the director of the Novato Institute for Somatic Research and Training. Somatics deals with the movement of our physical body and its relationship to our overall mental and physical health. Hanna often referred to what he called somatic amnesia or sensory motor amnesia. This is the neurological process where the brain forgets how to control muscles and how they relax.

Certain kinds of accidents, injuries, trauma, and stress can lead to habituated muscular dysfunction, or the habit of using our body in a less than resourceful way. We develop an inability to voluntarily control or relax muscles.

Through systematic exercises, the sensory-motor tracts of the brain and muscles are freed from these involuntary contractions and are taught to regain control. Somatic amnesia really comes down to not being aware of the position or feeling of our body. Awareness is the starting point.

The key in teaching the body to change our posture and alignment naturally and automatically is to first become aware of how it feels when we are using our physiology in a way that does not support our physical comfort and emotional states.

I want to take a moment to remind you that this works both ways; what we're thinking about eventually shifts our physiology, and the way we use our body powerfully influences what we are thinking. But how much will it change?

In one study, researchers actually altered the amount of physical energy people were able to put forth with their body by introducing a few simple thoughts. John Bargh, Mark Chen, and Lara Burrows gave thirty psychology students little word puzzles to complete. Half of the students had puzzles with words like "retired," "old," "careful," "shaky," and "ancient." The other half worked on puzzles with more neutral words. After completing the puzzle, the students were free to get up and go on with their day.

Unbeknownst to them, the researchers were timing how long it took each student to walk back to the elevator. Those who had worked on the puzzles with words related to older people took more time to get to the elevator. By seeing these few words related to the elderly, their brains had been primed in such a way that their behavior changed. They actually walked slower because of what they read.

How do you use your body? Are you stiff and inflexible? As you free up your body, you'll also be freeing your mind—not just metaphorically, but literally.

Many good forms of treatment can increase your flexibility. Is it just a coincidence that as people age and their body begins to stiffen, their thinking becomes more rigid as well? Give this reverse approach a try. At the very least, you'll find that it doesn't take as long to get out of bed, and that it doesn't hurt quite as much when you do.

In Closing

After you have read *The Productivity Epiphany* once, put it down somewhere for a couple of weeks. Then, every few days, read it for another five to ten minutes. You'll get something new every time for months to come. Things that weren't clear to you before will become clear. Things that were clear the first time around will become clearer. Let your mind work; this book is just a tool to trigger the brilliance within. Enjoy.

Bibliography

Andreas, Connirae. (2004). *NLP and Advanced Language Patterns*. Boulder, CO: NLP Comprehensive.

Andreas, Steve, and Charles Faulkner. (1996). *The New Technology of Achievement*. New York: Harper Collins.

Antion, Tom. (1999). *Wake 'Em Up! How to Use Humor and Other Professional Techniques to Create Alarmingly Good Business Presentations*. Landover Hills, MD: Anchor Publishing.

Austin, Andrew T. (2007). *The Rainbow Machine: Tales from a Neurolinguist's Journal*. Boulder, CO: Real People Press.

Byrne, Rhonda. (2006). *The Secret*. London: Atria Books. DVD.

Canfield, Jack. (2005). *The Success Principles: How to Get from Where You Are to Where You Want to Be*. New York: Collins.

Chandler, Steve. (2004). *100 Ways to Motivate Yourself: Change Your Life Forever*. Franklin Lakes, NJ: Career Press.

Childre, Doc, and Howard Martin. (2000). *The HeartMath Solution: The Institute of HeartMath's Revolutionary Program for Engaging the Power of the Heart's Intelligence*. San Francisco: HarperOne.

Ekman, Paul. (2003). *Emotions Revealed: Recognizing Faces and Feelings to Improve Communication and Emotional Life*. New York: Henry Holt.

Goleman, Daniel. (1995). *Emotional Intelligence: Why It Can Matter More Than IQ*. New York: Bantam Dell.

Gottman, John. (1995). *Why Marriages Succeed or Fail: And How You Can Make Yours Last*. New York: Simon & Schuster.

Hall, Michael L. (1996). *Dragon Slaying: Dragons into Princes*.

Grand Junction, CO: E. T. Publications.

Hanna, Thomas. (2004). *Somatics: Reawakening the Mind's Control of Movement, Flexibility, and Health.* Cambridge, MA: De Capo Books.

Hartley, Gregory, and Maryann Karinch. (2005). *How to Spot a Liar: Why People Don't Tell the Truth and How You Can Catch Them.* Franklin Lakes, NJ: Career Press.

Hogan, Kevin. (1996). *The Psychology of Persuasion: How to Persuade Others to Your Way of Thinking.* Gretna, LA: Pelican Publishing.

————. (2008). *The Secret Language of Business: How to Read Anyone in 3 Seconds or Less.* Hoboken, NJ: Wiley.

Howard, Vernon. (2001). *Psycho-Pictography: The New Way to Use the Miracle Power of Your Mind.* New Life Foundation.

Knowles, Eric S., and Jay A. Linn. (2003). *Resistance and Persuasion.* Mahwah, NJ: Lawrence Erlbaum.

Lieberman, David J. (2005). *How to Change Anybody.* New York: St. Martin's Press.

————. (2007). *You Can Read Anyone: Never Be Fooled, Lied to, or Taken Advantage of Again.* Lakewood, NJ: Viter Press.

Lindstrom, Martin. (2008). *Buy.ology: Truth and Lies about Why We Buy.* New York: Doubleday.

Maxwell, John C. (2005). *Today Matters: 12 Daily Practices to Guarantee Tomorrow's Success.* New York: Center Street.

Mortensen, Kurt W. (2004). *Maximum Influence: The 12 Universal Laws of Power Persuasion.* New York: Amacom.

Neill, Michael. (2006). *You Can Have What You Want: Proven Strategies for Inner and Outer Success.* Carlsbad, CA: Hay House.

Nightingale, Earl. (2007). *The Strangest Secret.* www.Bnpublishing.com.

Pease, Allen, and Barbara Pease. (2006). *The Definitive Book of Body Language.* New York: Bantam.

Reiman, Tonya. (2007). *The Power of Body Language.* New York: Pocket Books.

Reiss, Steven. (2002). *Who Am I? The 16 Basic Desires That Motivate and Define Our Personalities.* New York: Berkley Trade.

Rubino, Joe. (2003). *Restore Your Magnificence: A Life-Changing Guide to Reclaiming Your Self-Esteem.* Brooklyn, NY: Vision Works Publishing.

St. Clair, Carmen Bostic, and John Grinder. (2001). *Whispering in the Wind.* Scotts Valley, CA: J&C Enterprises.

Tracy, Brian. (2007). *Eat That Frog! 21 Great Ways to Stop Procrastinating and Get More Done in Less Time.* San Francisco: Berrett-Koelhler Publishers.

Trisler, Hank. (1986). *No Bull Selling: Winning Sales Strategy from America's Super Salesman.* New York: Random House Audio Publishing Group.

Vitale, Joe. (2006). *There's a Customer Born Every Minute: P.T. Barnum's 10 Rings of Power for Fame, Fortune, and Building an Empire.* Hoboken, NJ: Wiley.

————, and Ihaleakala Hew Len. (2007). *Zero Limits: The Secret Hawaiian System for Wealth, Health, Peace and More.* Hoboken, NJ: Wiley.

Vincent Harris

Speaker, Trainer, Seminar Leader

Vincent Harris is arguably one of the most exciting professional speakers in the world, capturing the attention of audience members and leaving them wanting more.

His keynote speeches, workshops, and seminars are described as "uplifting, entertaining, inspirational, and extremely informative." His audiences include Fortune 500 companies and virtually every size of business and association.

Call today for information on booking Vince to speak at your next meeting.

It's about Time—How to eliminate procrastination, ignite motivation, and get things done.

Facing Changes by Changing Faces—How to use the secrets of altering how you move your body to reduce stress instantly and access peak performance states.

Outstanding Customer Service—How to utilize verbal and nonverbal communication to create happier clients and customers.

Advanced Body Language—How to become a person of influence and use your nonverbal communication to communicate with precision.

Vince will customize his talk for your specific needs. Visit Harris Research International at www.vinceharris.com for more information, or call 660-204-4088 today for more information.

About the Author

Vincent Harris is a body language expert and the president and CEO of Harris Research International.

Vince's uncanny ability to detect the subtle but vital communication signals offered by others, and then use that information to help people rapidly achieve their goals, prompted one psychologist to give him the title of "The Human Whisperer."

As an international speaker, trainer, and consultant, he teaches men and women around the world to maximize their performance using leading-edge methods for making accelerated behavioral changes.